LIFESTYLE LAWYER REVOLUTION

LIFESTYLE LAWYER REVOLUTION

LIVE A LIFE YOU LOVE (WITHOUT LEAVING THE LAW!)

LAURA COWAN, Esq

Published by Best Seller Publishing®, St. Augustine, FL
Best Seller Publishing® is a registered trademark.
Printed in the United States of America.

ISBN: 978-1-966395-80-5

For more information, please write:
Best Seller Publishing®
1775 US-1 #1070
St. Augustine, FL 32084
or call 1 (626) 765-9750
Visit us online at: www.BestSellerPublishing.org

Disclaimer:

This book is intended to provide general information and insights on building and maintaining a "lifestyle" law practice. It is designed to assist attorneys in exploring alternative approaches to practicing law that may better align with their personal and professional goals. The content within this book is not a substitute for specific legal, financial, accounting, or business advice tailored to individual circumstances. The author and publisher make no representations or warranties regarding the accuracy, completeness, or current applicability of the information provided. It is the reader's responsibility to ensure compliance with all relevant legal and ethical requirements, including those governing attorney conduct, business practices, and client relations. Testimonials included in this book are from real students. However, to protect their privacy, names and identifying details may have been changed. These testimonials represent individual experiences, and the results described are unique to each person. There is no guarantee, expressed or implied, that you will achieve similar results or any results at all by purchasing this book. This book does not create an attorney-client relationship between the author and reader. The author and publisher disclaim any liability for any direct or indirect losses, damages, or risks that may arise from the use or reliance on the content of this book. The reader assumes full responsibility for any decisions made based on the information provided. All websites, links, and online resources mentioned in this book are accurate and functional at the time of publication. The author and publisher make no guarantee that the websites or resources referenced will remain accurate, available, or unchanged after the publication date. The author and publisher are not responsible for any changes, updates, or issues with the websites or links provided in this book. By reading this book, the reader acknowledges and agrees to the terms of this disclaimer.

Dedication

Dedicated to my father, James,
for encouraging me to Take Big Steps.

Acknowledgments

This book has been a labor of love, encouraged and supported by many people close to me. First and foremost, I'd like to thank Margaret McGrath. Without you, this book would not have been written. I would also like to thank Elizabeth Cowan Wright for her unwavering support. Not a day goes by when I don't feel immense gratitude for having you both as my big sisters. Mom would have been so proud.

And to my team, KC, Leighton, and Laney, I am so incredibly grateful for all your hard work and significant contributions to our community.

Finally, to my family of 2-Hour Lifestyle Lawyers — THANK YOU. This book is about you and for you. It has been an honor and a privilege to help you build your dreams.

Contents

Foreword

Carolyn Elefant

For over two decades, I've championed the cause of law firm ownership through my blog, MyShingle.com, and my own book, *Solo by Choice*. I've always believed that lawyers should have the option to chart their own course, own their talent, and build practices that align with their personal values and goals. Laura Cowan's book *Lifestyle Lawyer Revolution: Live a Life You Love (Without Leaving the Law!)* not only echoes these sentiments but provides a practical roadmap for achieving them.

Through a series of thoughtful exercises, Laura guides readers on a journey of self-discovery. She encourages lawyers to reflect on their personal values, define success on their own terms, and identify what truly brings meaning to their lives. This introspective process is crucial because it forms the foundation upon which lawyers can build a practice that serves their life rather than the other way around.

And what if you don't find your passion in law? Instead of walking away from it, Laura offers in this book a refreshing perspective: your work doesn't have to be your all-consuming passion. Instead, it can be a means to support the things that truly matter to you. This realistic approach is one of the book's greatest strengths.

One of the most valuable aspects of this book is its practical nature. Laura doesn't just leave readers with lofty ideas and aspirations. She provides concrete strategies and tools to turn those aspirations into reality. The section on technology is particularly noteworthy. In an age where digital competence is no longer optional, Laura offers a curated list of technology tools that can help lawyers streamline their practices from Day 1. This practical guidance is invaluable for those looking to start their own firms or optimize existing ones.

What sets *Lifestyle Lawyer Revolution* apart is its holistic approach to success. Laura understands that financial success, although important, is just one piece of the puzzle. She encourages readers to consider personal fulfillment, work-life balance, and overall well-being as equally important measures of success. This multifaceted view of success is refreshing and much needed in our profession.

The book also addresses a critical issue that many lawyers face: the fear of stepping out on their own. Through real-world examples and case studies, Laura demonstrates that it's possible to build a thriving practice while maintaining control over one's time and lifestyle. She doesn't sugarcoat the challenges, but she does provide the tools and mindset shifts necessary to overcome them.

As someone who has long advocated for lawyers to embrace entrepreneurship, I find Laura's approach both validating and inspiring. She doesn't just tell lawyers they can own their own firms; she shows them how to do it in a way that aligns with their personal values and goals. This is crucial because ownership without purpose can be just as unfulfilling as working for someone else.

The legal profession is at a crossroads. The traditional paths that once defined success are no longer the only options, nor are they necessarily the most fulfilling. *Lifestyle Lawyer Revolution* offers a timely alternative — a way for lawyers to leverage their skills and education to create lives and practices that truly resonate with who they are and what they want.

Carolyn Elefant
Founder, MyShingle.com

Introduction

If you always do what you've always done, you'll always get what you've always got.
— Henry Ford

If you always do what you've always done, you'll always be where you've always been.
— T. D. Jakes

Status Quo for You

Is This It?

That's the question Sarah, a 2-Hour Lifestyle Lawyer™ success story, asked each day before she suited up and went to work. She was one of the "lucky ones," a recent law school graduate who landed an associate position in litigation at a Big Law firm. She got the big salary and the bigger expectations: bill 2,000+ hours a year, long days, short (or non-existent weekends), and stress so intense her hair was falling out. As she dragged her exhausted self into the office on yet another Sunday morning, she found herself asking: *Is this it?*

Sarah reached a place I often hear on discovery and coaching calls: **I'm exhausted. I'm just so done. I'm burned out. I can't do this anymore.**

If you're not there (yet), do any of these statements resonate?

- I know what my values are, but I'm not living in alignment with them.
- I'm making a decent living, but I don't enjoy my life.
- The roles in my practice aren't properly delegated or understood. This costs me time, which costs me money.
- My technology is sometimes helpful but not as optimized as it could be. This *also* costs me time, which costs me money.
- AI (artificial intelligence) is going to take my job. I'm not sure how I can provide value in a profession where technology is changing so rapidly. I'm really discouraged.
- I'm an entrepreneur at heart, but managing a business while attending to my family is complicated.

These questions show up in different thoughts and different life and career stages for people, but the root is the same: **Is this it?**

Status Quo for the Law

If the statements above resonated, you are not alone. Research published by the American Addiction Centers[1] exploring the mental health situation in the legal profession indicates that lawyers suffer from higher rates of depression and anxiety and have greater rates of substance abuse problems than other professionals.

While depression affects around 7 percent of the U.S. adult population, **45 percent of lawyers report experiencing depression at some point during their careers.**

Of those who struggle with depression, almost **12 percent report experiencing suicidal thoughts.**

1 Priscilla Henson. "Addiction & Substance Abuse in Lawyers: Statistics to Know." American Addiction Centers (Updated June 21, 2024). https://americanaddictioncenters.org/workforce-addiction/white-collar/lawyers

A coexisting disorder like **depression, anxiety, and stress** magnifies the possibility of **using drugs or alcohol to cope** with the daily reality of practicing law.[2]

Approximately **one-third of lawyers report struggles with alcohol** that range from "problem drinking" to full-on alcohol abuse, a dependency that reportedly began either in law school or early in their career.

Nine percent of lawyers abuse prescription drugs, either to stay awake to work long hours or to sleep after a stressful day, week, month, or season. When combined with alcohol, abuse of prescription drugs can lead to deeper addiction or accidental overdose.

These are frightening statistics that paint a troubling picture of life as a lawyer. I'm not going to dispute that the practice of law is a stressful occupation. In fact, I'm going to go one step further and assert that, for many attorneys, **the practice of law is actually traumatizing.**

Big T Trauma vs Little T Trauma

Let's draw an important distinction about trauma because not all trauma (or individual responses to trauma) is the same. Elyssa Barbash, Ph.D., writing for *Psychology Today*, clarifies the difference between "big T" Trauma and "little t" trauma. She writes:

> Trauma is a deeply disturbing event that infringes upon an individual's sense of control and may reduce their capacity to integrate the situation or circumstances into their current reality. When most people think about trauma, they tend to think about those who have been exposed to war, combat, natural disasters, physical or sexual abuse, terrorism, and catastrophic accidents.

2 If you or someone you work with is experiencing depression, please seek out a licensed counselor or therapist. If you are experiencing suicidal thoughts, please seek help immediately. The International Association for Suicide Prevention's "Suicidal Crisis Support" page https://www.iasp.info/suicidalthoughts/ provides immediate assistance via talk or text. Or call 988 or visit the 988 Suicide & Crisis Lifeline at 988lifeline.org.

These are some of the most profound and, some may argue, the most debilitating experiences one can endure. However, a person does not have to undergo an overtly distressing event for it to affect them. *An accumulation of smaller or less pronounced events can still be traumatic, but in the small 't' form.* (emphasis mine)[3]

"Little t" trauma has only recently become a subject of research and reporting. It's harder to define because it happens over time and does not involve something we can easily point to, like a car accident or an assault. Prolonged interpersonal conflict, for example, can cause small t trauma, including divorce, custody issues, a prolonged legal battle, or chronic financial struggles. While "big T" Trauma creates an immediate and visceral sense of powerlessness and fear, "small t" trauma situations create an ongoing, pervasive, and difficult to pin down sense of helplessness. When "small t" trauma starts to accumulate, we often think, "My job is stressful, my marriage is in trouble, but this isn't 'traumatic.' It's just life."

Yes, it's life, and yes, over time, chronic, difficult situations can add up to "little t" trauma, which impacts your happiness and sense of security.

"Little t" Trauma and the Law

Who do people turn to for help in both "big T" and "little t" trauma situations? Doctors, first responders, and therapists are all frequent choices.

So are lawyers.

Irresolvable marital problems? Hire a lawyer.

3 Elyssa Barbash. "Different Types of Trauma: Small 't' versus Large 'T.' " *Psychology Today* (March 13, 2017). https://www.psychologytoday.com/us/blog/trauma-and-hope/201703/different-types-trauma-small-t-versus-large-t (Used with permission)

Custody issues? Hire a lawyer.

A prolonged legal battle over an injury or a work dispute? Hire a lawyer.

Chronic financial struggles? If they lead to bankruptcy ... hire a lawyer.

Let's consider another 2-Hour Lifestyle Lawyer (2HLL): Adam. Adam started his own firm right out of law school and has built a busy, lucrative practice in family law. For the last decade, he's been settling custody disputes and guiding his clients through divorce ... all the while at the mercy of opposing counsel, the court's schedule, and his clients' emotional turmoil. The father of two tweens, Adam found spending time with his children or socializing at parties — two things that used to nourish him — starting to feel like a burden. His spouse, kids, and friends have all commented on this change.

Adam's making enough money. His marriage isn't in trouble. His kids are doing well in school. His staff supports him effectively. And yet people have commented on the change in him, on his distance, his abruptness, his increasing inability to be present, patient, and attentive.

That's the consequence of "little t" trauma. Lawyers, by definition, step into the fray with people who have suffered both "big T" and "little t" trauma. **Due to the combative, contentious nature of the law and the win/lose structure of the outcomes, many lawyers live in a constant state of hyper-alertness, risking adrenal fatigue and burnout.** Your clients may win, and you may get paid, but you pay a price, physically, mentally, and emotionally, to stand in the trenches with your clients. When the matter ends, some clients respect your education and hard-won experience, are grateful for your services, and pay promptly. Others are not and do not.

Lawyers are ethically responsible for advocating for their clients, translating into laypersons' terms the often complicated and opaque legal system, ensuring the best possible outcome, and dealing with the fallout if that outcome does not happen. They counsel clients who are most likely facing a process they don't understand and where the outcome is uncertain. A sense of helplessness can be felt by both lawyer and client as they navigate the legal system. The judge, court schedule, and opposing counsel's tactics are all outside our control.

Frequently, I hear some variation of the "little t" trauma crisis from members of 2HLL:

- "I've been practicing family law for years, and **between my clients' situations and the court system, I'm burned out. I can't do it any more.**"
- "I was an associate in a litigation department at a law firm. I routinely worked until 2 a.m., went home to shower and change clothes, and returned to the office at 5 a.m. **That's not sustainable for me.**"
- "I'm a solo practitioner. **My family would be thrilled if I worked 40 hours a week because I'm working 80 now.**"
- "I've lost my sense of purpose. I don't know why I'm doing this anymore. **Some days I don't know why I'm doing anything anymore.**"
- "I'm a litigator, and I've had more than one **opposing counsel ruin a vacation** by filing a motion the evening before my family was supposed to leave."
- **"I'm disillusioned** when I solve a big problem for a client, then have to track them down them for payment, or send them to collections, or **when clients tell me my fees are 'highway robbery.'** "

These are the experiences of people who are struggling with "little t" trauma from living in a state of hyper-alertness that takes a physical toll on the body, one that sleep alone (if you are fortunate enough to be getting that suggested seven to eight hours a night) cannot repair. This puts you, the attorney, at risk for a long list of health problems, including anxiety, depression, high blood pressure, digestive issues, insomnia, headaches, and muscle and joint pain. You end up making choices that short-change your own mental, physical, and emotional well-being.

Additionally, your lived experience can be discounted, discouraging you from acknowledging the stress and "little t" trauma. Who hasn't heard comments like these:

- "What did you expect? That's why you went to law school, isn't it?"
- "Just leave work at work. How hard can it be?"
- "What's your hourly rate again? Don't complain to me when you're charging that much."

My Story and the 2-Hour Lifestyle Lawyer Solution

Stop doing what you've always done and being what you've always been, so you can get and be something more ...

I launched my law firm in the heart of New York City in 2016, diving headfirst into estate planning like everyone else: face-to-face, in person. Sure, we had the tech for virtual meetings (Zoom's been around since 2013), but let's be real—it wasn't "socially acceptable." Nobody was dropping $5,000 on an estate plan without first shaking your hand at the office. If you wanted to make it in this business, you met with clients in person, 9 a.m.–5 p.m., Monday through Friday, and worked nights and weekends. That was the game.

Then March 2020 hit.

New York City shut down overnight. I moved to Rhode Island to quarantine with my Dad, and I'll never forget sitting at his kitchen table, staring at my laptop, thinking, "How the heck am I going to get clients now?" It was terrifying. No roadmap, no precedent, just bills that needed paying.

So, I got to work.

Educational seminars became webinars. Client meetings? Zoom calls. The ubiquitous office whiteboard turned into a shared Excel sheet. Contracts were signed online, payments processed by credit card.

Every single step of my practice had to be rethought, retooled, and revamped. And it needed to be done quickly because I still had Manhattan rent to pay. When the dust settled, I had something entirely new: **an A–Z roadmap to a fully virtual estate planning practice, battle-tested in the legal trenches of New York City.** And as the world began to wake up, I noticed a trend. Lawyers everywhere were asking, "How can I do virtual estate planning?"

Enter the 2-Hour Lifestyle Lawyer.

The 2-Hour Lifestyle Lawyer is a reflection of my post-COVID reality: $10,000+/month in revenue from serving clients virtually and working only a couple of hours per day. It is my answer to the "new normal." A normal where part-time lawyers are the rule, not the exception. Where the advice given from a Parisian café is just as powerful as what you'd get in a boardroom. Where technology isn't the enemy, but the ally that gives us our time back, letting us focus on what really matters. A new normal that delivers five-star service to clients, even if you're only serving a few each month. **A normal that lets you live a life you love without leaving the law.**

... a life I **love**, you say?

Yes. More fulfilled. More connected. More relaxed. More engaged. More in control. How does that sound?

Let's face facts: Law school doesn't ask you (and wasn't intended to ask you) what you want out of life. It doesn't prepare you to run your own business, navigate the hierarchy and politics of a big firm, or convert leads into clients. It doesn't prepare you to send clients to collection agencies or to handle them when they start screaming at you about something over which you have no control. It doesn't prepare you for a lead who won't fill out a questionnaire or who cancels their meeting at the last minute after you've booked a babysitter. I could go on and on. These are all things that add to "little t" trauma.

The 2-Hour Lifestyle Lawyer program doesn't treat the *symptoms* of "little t" trauma. Instead, it treats the root cause of dissatisfaction with the legal profession: the overworking as a badge of honor, the chronic state of hyper-alertness that destroys your mental health and eats away at whatever self-care you're able to manage, the billable hours dilemma that ensures you get paid but also saps any sense of flow and connection you have, and the drift that likely started in law school away from your values to the values others say matter.

At 2-Hour Lifestyle Lawyer, you are supported through the process of exploring what **you** want out of life, your current reality, and a way forward based on a proven, tested path to a career that serves you rather than you serving it.

In the post-pandemic environment we now live in, we show you how to capitalize on AI, technology, and team-based solutions that get you out of the trenches and into a life you love.

We help you develop a full and attentive relationship with your energy and your time: How **you** regain control of how you spend it and bill for it, how technology and well-defined support roles can take back **your** time, and how **you** implement tools and strategies to spend it in a way that feels meaningful to **you**.

Not me.

You.

The premise of 2HLL is that **you** decide what "success" looks and feels like. You decide if you work 10 hours a week to support your family or 90. You decide if you want to work virtually or from an office (or a combination of the two!) You decide if you want to meet with clients every day of the week or just on Tuesdays and Wednesdays. You decide if you want to serve two clients per month or twenty. I'm not here to tell you how to live your life or structure your practice. **I am here to show you that options exist.**

A 2-Hour Lifestyle Lawyer is a lawyer who has chosen to define success in a different way from the way she (or he, or they) thought she had to when she graduated from law school. A 2-Hour Lifestyle Lawyer has chosen to build their own path, to serve the populations and communities they want to serve while utilizing technology, appropriate staffing, and time management tools to maximize their productivity, work the hours they want to work, and provide excellent client service.

In short, a 2-Hour Lifestyle Lawyer is a lawyer who lives a life they love without leaving the law.

What's Next?

In the upcoming chapters, I'll explore foundational 2HLL concepts and discuss how Sarah, Adam, and other students capitalized on the membership to rebuild their careers and their lives. You'll learn from other members' experiences and see the results of their efforts in the program.

Part One — How 2HLL Brings Clarity and Alignment

In Chapter One, you'll take stock of where you are now and where you want to be by excavating your **Why** from under all your responsibilities.

In Chapter Two, I'll demonstrate how 2HLL focuses on your **lived experience**, not social media representations.

In Chapter Three, you'll identify your **values** and see how 2HLL can bring you into closer alignment with them.

Why do I start here? Because without a solid foundation, change is most often superficial and temporary. Reconnecting with your **Why** for your business and your personal lives frames how you define success. **How you define success** is influenced by your values (and derailed by living by someone else's definition of success). Identifying and bringing forward your values **reduces that sense of misalignment that comes from chronic "little t" trauma.**

Part Two — How 2HLL Transforms Your Law Practice, and You

This section will help you reclaim your autonomy and your agency.

In Chapter Four, I'll talk about how 2HLL **turns traditional billing on its head** and supercharges your best chance for making money while providing excellent services to your clients and community.

In Chapter Five, I'll address how the **dreaded billable hour** actually holds you back, and how 2HLL supports you in leaving it behind.

In Chapter Six, we explore 2HLL's **Tech Stack**, a vital component of the 2HLL framework, including my thoughts on why the current "the sky is falling!" attitude to AI is misguided at best and damaging at worst.

In Chapter Seven, I'll give 2HLL's guidance on why **building a team** is one of the most important steps you can take beyond *Is this it?*

Along the way, I'll offer **exercises** to support you as you explore how 2HLL can help you into a life you love without leaving the law.

This is 2-Hour Lifestyle Lawyer. **Welcome aboard the Lifestyle Lawyer Revolution!**

Let's start by diving into a simple question that, if explored thoughtfully over time, can yield profound results: What's your Why?

Chapter Summary

- Practicing law can lead to an ongoing sense of helplessness that leads to "little t" trauma.
- This manifests in varying levels of stress, burnout, and addiction, aka more helplessness.
- The 2-Hour Lifestyle Lawyer offers you a path to alleviate helplessness by taking control of every area of your practice.

Visit lifestylelawyerrevolution.com for free resources!

Part One

How 2HLL Brings Clarity and Alignment

One
What's Your Why?

A successful life is one that is lived through understanding and pursuing one's own path, not chasing after the dreams of others.
— Chin-Ning Chu

Your time is limited, so don't waste it living someone else's life. Don't be trapped by dogma — which is living with the results of other people's thinking.
— Steve Jobs

Taking Stock

Remember Sarah, my 2HLL member from the Introduction? Sarah grabbed the brass ring right out of law school, with a job in litigation at a Big Law firm. As a fourth-year associate, she was making $310,000 per year, yet found herself asking each long, long day, "Is this it?" When a question like this surfaces in your consciousness, the first step isn't to make a snap judgment, then set some goals based on the impulse of the moment. **The first step is to reflect.**

In my experience, coaching almost 500 lawyers in the 2HLL model, there are several steps that members need to take early in the program that create an underpinning based on the unique elements of who you are. During that process, you start at the very beginning and assess where you are, look back on how you got there, and consider where you thought you would be. This is a vital step because the process of reflecting reveals insights and opportunities that might not surface in the day-to-day.

Having some clarity around where you came from, where you are right now, and where you want to be is the first step towards building a buffer between you and the daily "little t" trauma of life as a lawyer. Equally important, the decision Sarah faced — whether or not to leave a guaranteed Big Law salary along with all the perks and prestige — wasn't one she took lightly. In addition to the paycheck, after three years of law school, a clerkship, and several years as an associate, Sarah's sense of self was tied up in what she thought a "good lawyer" was.

The question is ... who defined a "good lawyer" for her?

What Exactly Is a "Good Lawyer"?

Grab a brand new legal pad (yellow is fine; pink works, too!) or get out your tablet's pencil because we're offering several exercises throughout this book, and they build on each other. Let's begin.

EXERCISE:

Does this definition of a "good lawyer" resonate with you?

- A "good lawyer" is someone who **works all the time**, wearing the "I'm so busy" badge with honor.

- A "good lawyer" is someone who is **an associate for a big, well-known firm and is billing 2000+ hours a year on the way to making partner.**
- A "good lawyer" **makes a lot of money.**
- A "good lawyer" **honors the tradition** of the profession, is **competitive** to the point of viciousness, **buries their opponent** in a mountain of paper, and fights their way out from under the mountain of paper that opposing counsel sent over.
- A "good lawyer" is **always ready to take a client's call after hours, *and*** on the weekend, ***and*** on vacation. (Boundaries, anyone?)
- A "good lawyer" **never misspells a word** or uses a comma rather than a period and has an immediate answer for every question their clients ask.

Does that sound like a description of a human being who practices law or a suit-wearing, brief-writing robot? How do you feel when you read that description? (I felt exhausted and anxious just writing it!)

Take a moment and notice what's happening in your body, heart, and mind when you conjure up your own image of a "good lawyer."

EXERCISE:

1. How do you define a "good lawyer?"
2. Where did you get the idea of what it means to be a "good lawyer"? Movies? TV? Books? A friend or family member? Your law school colleagues?
3. Can you meet this definition with your current life circumstances? How do you feel when you reflect on this?

Let's explore this a little further.

Your Why Then

With that awareness clearly in mind, let's go back to that momentous (and expensive) decision that set you on the path to law school. Take a few moments in a quiet environment and reflect on the following questions.

EXERCISE:

1. Why did you go to law school? What did you hope for? Dream of? How did you want to feel? (Honesty is key here.)
2. What experiences or individuals influenced your decision? Were these influences positive or negative? Helpful or unhelpful? Are they the same individuals or experiences who define what a "good lawyer" is for you?
3. What circumstances were foremost in your life at the time?

Your answer may be lofty and ambitious, moving towards something, or based on a need for security by moving away from something. Sarah, for example, and like many of our members, went to law school to secure the financial future she wanted in precisely the way she did — obtaining that Big Law job. But members chose law school for a wide variety of reasons. Below are a few 2HLL members' responses to that question. How do these reasons resonate with or clarify your own thoughts?

- "I wanted a job that would be **meaningful and not leave me bored.** I was very analytical by nature and had strong arguing skills, so I pursued a career as a litigator."
- "To be honest, I went to law school to **avoid entering the workforce** and to try to **find a direction.**"
- "I grew up in a home where **my mom worked three jobs and we still struggled financially** ... This primed me for wanting a better life ..."
- "I have wanted to go to law school since I was in elementary school after a **field trip to the courthouse.**"
- "I always wanted to **help others** and believed that law school would allow me to do that."
- "Access a profession to **provide for my family.**"
- "I was **fired from a Legal Secretary position** I had held for 10 years. At that time, I only had [an] AA degree ... I was in my 30s, married and with two children."

And finally, the most concise answer (and my own personal favorite):

- "Indoor work." (For the record, that's all this individual said in their survey response, and they are still practicing — inside — decades later.)

Most answers boil down to a variation of "Given the experiences I'd had and what I knew at the time, it seemed like a good idea." You felt a need, or a want, or a calling. You wanted to avoid a situation or possibility (e.g., outdoor work or boredom). Law school met the criteria to move you forward. You applied, got in, and graduated with a degree and (probably) student loan debt that varied from negligible to manageable to absolutely crushing.

Based on your law school experience and results, as well as your financial responsibilities, you then got a job. Maybe you struck out on your own right away or worked in a mid-sized firm. Maybe you landed that top prize that Sarah landed: a clerkship or a Big Law associate position. Either way, as life has happened in the intervening years, it's possible, even likely, that the Why that sent you to law school is not the same Why that's motivating you now.

Your Why Now

Reflect on and answer the following questions as honestly as possible to reflect on your own journey as you've worked as a lawyer.

EXERCISE:

1. What are your hopes, dreams, and constraints now? It may help to call to mind the following:
    - changes in your personal/familial life
    - your financial situation
    - living arrangements (moves, home ownership)
    - your health
    - other responsibilities
2. How do you feel at work? Is this different from how you would like to feel? How does your current work environment move you toward your hopes and dreams?

3. Reflect on your daily lived experience. Do you feel like you experience meaningful work, like you belong to a tribe you respect, and are contributing to your community in a way that aligns with your values?
4. Who or what is currently influencing your career trajectory in the law? Identify any voices that aren't your own. This could include parents, friends, partners (personal or professional), social media, colleagues, or others.

Whys change. Adam, another case study and member I'm following through this book, went to law school because he was intrigued by how the analytical nature of the work blended with the ability to help people. He started his own firm shortly after passing the bar. However, 15 years later, he has two children in middle school, and the day when they transition into their own adult life, either through college or work, feels much closer than it used to. He's more aware of time passing and how little of it he's spent with his children.

What To Do With This Information?

I'm not going to lie: this process can be really disheartening. The difference between the responses to the above exercises can be summed up as the difference between what you see on social media and your daily life. (More on that in the next chapter.) Many lawyers dislike their work and their work environments. When they take stock of reality (student loan debt, business costs, a mortgage or rent, a car payment (or two), familial responsibilities for children and aging parents, and so on), they feel discouraged, stuck, even hopeless. Their reality can be summed up in the following way: *I can't change anything about what's going on in my current life, and it's depressing to think about how adrift and, at the same time, trapped I am. Why even bother thinking about it?*

Why? **Because change is possible, and you don't have to live life and practice law the way you or the world thought you should five, ten, or twenty years ago.**

The 2-Hour Lifestyle Lawyer program supports this premise.

Our Signature Course is the blueprint for a post-COVID estate planning practice: one that is virtual or hybrid, offers flexibility and a reasonable schedule for the lawyer, and provides five-star service to its clients. One that would not have been possible even five years ago.

We teach lawyers how to become leaders in their communities by hosting educational seminars and webinars. We share our secrets on converting cold leads to warm leads and warm leads to clients in a consultation generating fees of $2,000–$6,000 per estate plan. We show you how to deliver five-star service while automating as much of the process as possible — all within a supportive, nurturing community of entrepreneur-lawyers. Our Lifestyle Lawyer Collective™ membership provides ongoing coaching and marketing for graduates of the program.

Let's be very clear here. The 2HLL model does not mean that you overcharge for your services and then do bad work, all to be able to sit on the beach. The model I teach emphasizes excellence in every aspect of your practice, from ongoing community education through efficiency and process improvements that benefit you and your clients to networking in a way that creates even more value for you, your business partners, and your community.

That's the 2HLL way.

Why 2-Hour Lifestyle Lawyer?

You are not alone! I asked 2HLL members to reflect on what's changed since their original decision to go to law school and why they chose 2HLL to get them moving forward.

Burnout in other practice areas was both a common Why and reason for enrolling in 2-Hour Lifestyle Lawyer:

- **"I left the legal profession for several years**. I realized after many years away that I missed the practice of law ... I thought long and hard about what I wanted my practice to look like before stepping back in. **I wanted to help with legacy building in my community**. Estate planning seemed like a great fit. I [learned about 2HLL] ... I liked the concept and here I am."
- "I am a reforming trial lawyer ... Most of the time I was overwhelmed with loads and loads of emails and document dumps as part of endless discovery. **We basically litigated**

cases in the discovery disputes. I didn't find it fun or rewarding. Also, the hours I worked and the little reward in pay for the risk of taking on contingency fee cases, was just not worth it."

- "... certain demanding **clients were driving me nuts** ..."
- "My current practice consists of mostly **court appointed child advocacy work in juvenile court and it is emotionally draining** ... COVID also taught me that **spending more quality time with my son who is growing up too quickly was very important to me**. 2HLL was an eye opening gift! It made me see that there was a way **I could still use my law degree, make great money, and ... have the ability to do all the things with my family that I wanted to**. More importantly, I could still provide something valuable to my clients without them emotionally draining me."

Some members joined to better manage their firm:

- "**Running a law firm is difficult and expensive** and I thought I could learn about how to ... make this possible and manageable."
- "I wanted to **automate my practice** ... "
- "I started doing some estate planning and probate in 2020, but it wasn't my sole focus. In spring of 2023, I decided to stop doing criminal defense and family law and focus only on estate planning and probate. **I was looking for guidance on how to promote my firm, learn more than the basics, set up my systems, etc.**"

Others wanted to boost their income in a transformative way:

- "**I also am feeling very burnt out in my current practice area**. Child welfare law, while very important, is an extremely [emotionally] heavy practice area. Most of my work is currently appointed cases. My state has one of the **lowest compensation rates in the country**."

Many, many folks wanted the flexibility to work when and where they wanted to:

- "I am searching for a way to practice law while not sacrificing what is most important to me, my family. **I became a mother 2 years ago, and at that moment my priorities shifted**. I want to work to live, not live to work."
- "I was looking ... to **start my own practice and create a lucrative practice without the billables.** I needed **flexibility to operate an office from home and work remotely**."
- "I wanted to create a life for myself where I could enjoy my work and still have a life outside of it. **I was burned out after post-COVID life of hyper-balancing work and family, working on other people's schedules, and producing results that others reaped the benefits of, leaving me tired and unexcited**. I wanted to be my own boss, create my own schedule with full autonomy, look forward to working, and solve problems that touch real people."
- **"I wanted to have control over my schedule and not be stuck at the mercy of a court's schedule and my client's emergency matters**. I wanted to be guaranteed pay — and not working on the hope of getting paid if I won. I wanted to not have to wake up in the middle of the night worrying about an angry client going through a difficult time and taking it out on me."
- "I had just opened my own practice after 21 years in practice. **My children have since moved out and my husband and I are finally empty nesters. I wanted independence and autonomy** to make my own business decisions, run my practice the way I wanted to run it and have a flexible schedule."

Finally, many of my members wanted support and a community in which to learn and grow:

- "I loved how [2HLL] strived to help people make the career of law work for them, not the other way around."
- "I was seeking a **community of like-minded entrepreneur attorneys,** and to learn more about this field of law, but within the parameters of an interactive and supportive community ... **The community [and] supportive and caring leadership** is primarily what makes a huge difference! That is what I was looking for as a solo practitioner."
- "I stumbled upon 2HLL, and it was the best fit for me in terms of what the course covers, affordability, timing, etc., plus **Laura is such a positive and reassuring presence that I CAN do this!**"
- "I never practiced after law school (I took a nontraditional job and then became a SAHM). **I [wanted] a mentor to help me figure out setting up my own practice so I can serve my community.**"
- "I joined Carolyn Elefant's AI Accelerator and heard Laura speak. I knew instantly this was something I was searching for. **The knowledge and community are unmatched, and I no longer feel like I'm doing this new thing all alone.**"

What Makes 2HLL Unique?

First, the process works. As one member said:

> I had been a stay-at-home mom to two kiddos for five years when I found 2HLL. My youngest was going to start preschool in the fall, so toward the end of summer, I began to explore what I wanted to do when I finally would have some time to do something for me. I had not worked outside the home for the past

> five years and felt like I was starting from square one. I made a plan [and] supplemented my 2HLL training with a self-directed intensive of Wealth Counsel's CLEs. **I found 2HLL in June and before the end of July, I had signed my first two clients.**

She recouped her initial investment in the program and her first year's operating costs in six weeks! (NOTE: This member is now enjoying $10,000 WEEKS!)

Second, I am so proud of the community we've built. It's one of the most valuable benefits of membership. The community is growing and diverse, inclusive and supportive, and coming from a place of optimism, not fear. We have folks who want to make an impact in their local community and others who want to read by the beach. We have deeply religious individuals from a variety of faiths who see their legal practice as a spiritual calling and others who just need to pay their bills. We have 30-year practitioners looking for a new challenge and newer attorneys who are juggling work, home, and the school schedule and calendar, all from the minivan while driving to their kids' extracurricular activities. We even have law school students in the course and new attorneys waiting for their bar results!

Whoever you are, no matter your Why, our community is here for you.

Third, 2HLL gives you an intangible yet necessary quality: freedom. Some of our 2HLL practitioners want to build a seven-, eight-, or nine-figure law firm. Many don't! Some use our consultation script mostly unchanged; others take bits and pieces. The most frequently mentioned reasons behind choosing 2HLL are the **freedom to set your own schedule, the freedom to be around for your families or interests, and the freedom to practice law in a way that serves you and your law firm, not Laura Cowan and the 2-Hour Lifestyle Lawyer brand.**

Finally, and most importantly, **the 2HLL special sauce is our team's commitment to your success as *you* define it. Everyone at 2HLL wants to help you reach your Why for your unique situation.** If you want to build a seven-figure firm, we're here for that. If you want to serve two clients a month and make art, we're here for that. The business scales up or down based on YOU, not based on what we've created or what we envision.

Sarah and Adam

Let's revisit two of my case studies. Sarah, one of my Big Law survivors, found after completing these exercises that her Why had totally shifted in the face of the reality of a Big Law job. **Her new Why: Learn how to run her own firm so she's earning Big Law money without the Big Law demands.**

Adam's new Why? Get control of his schedule so he can spend more time with his children before they leave home. For him, the remaining years with his kids provided the impetus to shift from a draining practice area to one that supported him and his family on every level.

Are you curious about *my* Why? It may surprise you.

I support entrepreneurial attorneys because starting my own law firm transformed my life, and I want to help other lawyers step beyond their fears and discover the incredible opportunities that await them as lawyer-entrepreneurs.

I'll share more details about my past and what drove me to launch 2-Hour Lifestyle Lawyer a little later! But for now, getting back to our members' responses, you may have noticed that none of them include comments like, "I have a passion for estate planning that transcends any other area of law," or "It is my life's purpose to prepare Revocable Living Trusts for my community." And that's okay! **In the next chapter, I'll dive into the "passion" fallacy and how 2HLL sets you up for a meaningful career that supports your life.**

Have you identified your Why? If not, revisit the exercises earlier in the chapter to reflect and feel what's bothering you and what gives you energy, and even hope. **Once you've identified your Why, we'll turn our attention to Reality and how the 2HLL program and adapting your mindset can shift your reality**. I'll also dive deeper into my story and share how getting fired (yes, fired!) inspired me to hang my own shingle in search of the level of meaning and contribution I aspired to and was lacking in my life.

Chapter Summary

- You don't have to practice, define success, or live the way you thought a "good lawyer" lives when you came out of law school.
- It's vital to find your Why. Reflecting on the decisions you've made and your current life circumstances provides a necessary foundation for moving forward with your career and, ultimately, your life.
- 2HLL Members come from a variety of backgrounds and situations.
- They are unified in their desire for more freedom, a more efficient practice, and a roadmap to both.

Visit lifestylelawyerrevolution.com for free resources!

Two
The Cage Match Among Your Why, Social Media, and Reality

Without work, all life goes rotten. But when work is soulless, life stifles and dies.
— Albert Camus

I never dreamt of success. I worked for it.
— Estée Lauder

Start where you are. Use what you have. Do what you can.
— Arthur Ashe

It's impossible to be perfect, and you won't do a good job if you're too focused on proving yourself to others.
— Jessica Williams

I'm Not Measuring Up

"I spend hours each week on social media and all I see are people who seem to have perfect lives, or lawyers who seem to have it all. It's such a waste of time, and when I put my phone down, I'm so demoralized I don't even dare to dream about making a change."

Lenore, another of our 2HLL members, shared her experience on a coaching call of trying to define what she wants her life and practice to look like while swimming in a sea of influencer content. I've never had so many fellow participants on a Zoom call hit the thumbs-up button in solidarity. We all get messages, overt and more subtle, about what it means to live a meaningful life and to be of value. So let's tease some of these messages out into the light and take a close look at them, starting with everyone's favorite maxim: follow your passion, and you'll never work a day in your life.

But ... What About Passion?

I'm going to let you in on a little secret: my passion in life isn't centered on estate planning. If I reach back to my childhood for career direction, I'd still be taking ballet class six days a week and dancing the Dew Drop Fairy in *The Nutcracker* (a girl can dream, right?)

Given that I unfortunately do not meet the body type requirements for classical ballet, I would also be destitute and chronically disappointed with my life and my options.

Why am I telling you this?

Because you don't need to be passionate about your work in order to have a lucrative, meaningful career. In fact, insisting that feeling emotionally connected to your job is vital to happiness and success can actually be harmful.

Often, lawyers have too many financial responsibilities and people depending on them to walk away from a potentially lucrative career in the law. Often, those same lawyers are unhappy in their work. **The solution to the "little t" trauma of a law career isn't to start loving the law or any other career (we do not recommend trying to love something that can't love you back and is intentionally or unintentionally harming your mental, physical, and emotional health).** That's not what 2HLL offers because **I don't think you don't have to love your job**, much less feel passionate about it.

The 2HLL solution is to make your career work for you so you can enjoy your life. That's success.

No romance required. This isn't personal. It's business.

That's why the opening quotes for this chapter don't include a component of "do what you love and the money will follow." That's the social media version of career direction, where your stylist and your makeup artist and your photographer and lighting designer and your set designer and your paralegal and virtual assistant and golden retriever all conspire to make the work of an estate planning lawyer seem like something straight out of an influencer's social media posts.

2HLL lives in reality. Your reality.

Reality

You've clarified your Why. Maybe it's spending time with your family, building your business, or reducing the stress you feel on a daily basis. In cases of career dissatisfaction, we're often told that the next step is to find a career you love, something you feel passionate about, and do that. "You'll never work a day in your life!"

Having a lofty Why feels great ... until the next phone call from a concerned or anxious client, opposing counsel files a motion right before a holiday weekend, or the court sets a trial date right in the middle of your already-booked family vacation. Although it's important, and sometimes fun, to create a vision board around a life based on a lofty Why, it's not enough to create meaningful, real-world change. Anyone who's tried to stick to a diet on Donut Fridays at the office knows that motivation and energy can disintegrate in the face of daily life: bills to pay, children to raise, parents to care for, homes and cars to maintain, golden retrievers to walk, all with the ongoing "little t" trauma of daily life as a lawyer.

The 2HLL approach gets that. I carefully designed the course to support you in making the transition from a less-palatable reality to one aligned with your Why. It's been that way since Day 1 because the program grew out of *my* pretty awful reality.

Laura's Reality

I claimed my Why during the worst four-week stretch of my life.

In March of 2015, my mother died unexpectedly.

On April 1, 2015 (yes, April Fool's Day), I was fired from the highly paid, prestigious job I'd left the law to take.

Death, grief, and anger have a way of clarifying our thinking. In the aftermath of my life completely crumbling on multiple levels, I realized that although I'd had high-status jobs in a number of fields, including stints with Ernst & Young and Goldman Sachs, I wasn't living up to my full potential. I knew I was capable of so much more than what my nine-to-five offered, and I was tired of trying to squeeze myself into the corporate mold. Rather than seek out another position working to fulfill someone else's dream, it was time for me to start making my own come true. I took some time off, moved to Italy, and took stock of my life. It wasn't long before I made the decision to open my own law firm. By 2016, I'd opened the Law Office of Laura Cowan, a boutique estate planning practice in the heart of New York City.

Sounds like a social media fantasy, right? It wasn't.

Lest you think I'd amassed two years' worth of savings and a healthy retirement account to rely on while I made this transition, here's a little more unfiltered, out-in-the-sunlight truth behind my journey to my career as an estate planning attorney and entrepreneur: it started with a bunch of **zeroes**.

I had **zero** clients.

I had **zero** real-world knowledge of estate planning.

I had **zero** financial safety net.

The only numbers bigger than zero was the **six-figure balance of my student loan debt** for law school, the **mid-four figure monthly rent** on my Manhattan apartment, and the number of attorneys in Manhattan with degrees from the best law schools in the country, working for the best-known firms in the city, aka my **competition**.

Was I helpless? No.

I had other, less tangible qualities that helped me overcome the zeroes. Grit. Motivation (an empty bank account and no paycheck is highly motivating). Over ten years of knowledge of law, accounting, and business management amassed in my prior positions. A strong, interior-felt sense that if I kept on working for someone else, putting MY energy into THEIR dream, my soul would shrivel up and die.

But mostly **Grit**. (More on that, and other values, in the next chapter.)

In our experience, I am not an unusual 2HLL. Most of my members do not have their ducks neatly paddling in rows. Although I have members who come to 2HLL with positive asset balances and good health, others, like Sarah, are in debt. Others, like Adam, have children at home along with a mortgage or rent payments. Some are living with or caring for a parent or partner with a chronic or terminal illness. Most are exhausted in mind, body, and heart. All are trying very hard to do the best they can with the resources they have.

What Decades of Research and Expert Analysts Say About Work Satisfaction

Feeling exhausted and burned out is where the passion fallacy usually surfaces. The hypothesis of the passion fallacy, supported by both traditional media and social media, follows this (il)logical train of thought:

Burned out at work? Do what you love, and you'll never work a day in your life, and the money will flow!

But, according to Cal Newport, a computer scientist, writer, and world-renowned thought leader in productivity and meaning spaces, social science research into work satisfaction doesn't bear out this hypothesis.

After he completed his Ph.D. and post-doctoral fellowship at MIT, Newport went on the job market for what he hoped was the first and last time, seeking a tenure-track position at a university. Consequently, he was curious about what qualities and conditions were necessary for people to feel satisfied at work and set out to research this question. You can read the in-depth results of his research and conclusions in his 2012 book *So Good They Can't Ignore You;* here, I'll summarize the conclusion because it is the complete antithesis to the passion fallacy, especially as it shows up on social media.

Newport's research found that the best science on feeling motivated is based on Self-Determination Theory (SDT). Your work (and this holds in other areas of your life as well) should "fulfill three basic psychological needs ... to feel intrinsically motivated," which he defined as follows:

- **Autonomy:** the feeling that you have control over your day and that your actions are important.
- **Competence:** the feeling that you are good at what you do.
- **Relatedness:** the feeling of connection to other people.[4]

Although feeling passionate about your work can lead to these feelings, the good news for lawyers struggling with "little t" trauma is that passion is not required to create and enjoy these feelings. You don't have to climb Mount "I Love the Law and Feel Passionate About It." With intentional thought and effort, these needs can be met in nearly every

4 Cal Newport. *So Good They Can't Ignore You: Why Skills Trump Passion in the Quest for Work You Love* (New York: Business Plus, 2018), p. 18.

career. **With 2HLL, members can intentionally and systematically reduce the "little t" trauma helplessness inherent in many practice areas by implementing the processes, systems, and workflows that increase autonomy and competence and create a connection to others.**

With a virtual estate planning practice, you regain control over your schedule and your work location (autonomy).

You provide a vital service to your clients and create connections both in your community and the 2HLL community (competence and relatedness).

You master the intricacies of estate planning (competence).

More control over your time and energy means you have more left in your tank to be in a deep and meaningful relationship with family, friends, and yourself (autonomy, competence, and relatedness).

Newport emphasizes that creating a career that meets these psychological needs requires focusing on building what he calls "capital" in relevant areas. This includes the meaningful content of your job — your legal expertise — but also includes other arenas. In the case of 2HLL, it includes, among other things, developing as an entrepreneur, understanding and committing to marketing the services you provide, and deepening your capacity to build relationships.

The bad news is that a transition like this is not a "one-and-done" event.

The good news is that it's not a "one-and-done" event.

Perfection is not required out of the gate, or ever. You're in control. You get many chances to experiment, explore, and refine, building knowledge and capital that rewards **you**, not someone else. I encourage excellence, not perfection.

The How

Think back to the point made in the Introduction regarding what characterizes "little t" trauma: an ongoing, pervasive, and difficult-to-pin-down sense of helplessness. The antidote to helplessness is both ephemeral (hope) and practical — intentionality. **The 2HLL program is built on Intentionality.**

What does practicing or living intentionally mean?

Ryder Carroll, the creator of the Bullet Journal, argues that time management and, therefore, the very building blocks of our lives depend on Intentionality. His definition has proven helpful to 2HLL members:

An intention is a commitment to a process.

Not a dream, or a wish, or a resolution, or an ambition, or a vision board, or a "someday maybe" vague thought.

Once you start looking, you see your life is full of processes: the process of raising children, running a business, drafting a will or trust, billing clients, maintaining a home, and nurturing relationships. Setting an intention provides a direction and structure for your weeks and days — and your goals. Approaching your practice as a lawyer with Intentionality ensures that no matter how chaotic the work day is or how unhappy you are, you're engaging with your career and your life from the driver's seat, not the back seat (or worse, locked in the trunk).

This is where the 2HLL rubber meets the reality road, and it's why passion often isn't enough to get you through the intentional process of adding a practice area, shifting out of one practice area and into another, starting your own firm, or streamlining the processes and workflows in your existing practice.

Once you know your Why, setting intentions to support that Why provides a framework for how you make decisions. If your Why, like Sarah's, is to make Big Law money without working Big Law hours, then your intentions — the processes you commit to — should support that. Perhaps that means you commit to refining your marketing process to get more potential clients into your sales funnel. Or, if your Why, like Adam's, is to spend more time with your children in the few years before they leave home, then your inefficient intake and appointment management process needs attention because it's costing you valuable hours each week.

Keeping the intentions you have set can be difficult in today's world of non-stop distractions. Remember Lenore's experience with social media, a chronic feeling of wasted time and not measuring up? The apps on our phones are intentionally designed to keep us coming back to them more often than we want and to keep us looking at the screen for longer than we intended. Unless you have carefully curated your feeds, you are being fed advertisements and suggestions to look at or follow based on what data has been collected about you. I'll talk more about this in chapter 6, which addresses Technology.

With that in mind, set your phone aside and work through the following exercise.

EXERCISE:

1. Keeping in mind both your personal and professional life and Carroll's definition of an intention as a "commitment to a process," what intentions have you set, consciously or unconsciously?
2. Who do those intentions belong to? You? Your family? Your colleagues?
3. Who do those intentions support — mentally, financially, emotionally, physically? Include yourself in this!
4. Do these intentions support your autonomy, competence, and connectedness?

2HLL Intentionality

When I started my estate planning practice in 2016, I was very intentional about everything from marketing to developing and refining my knowledge of estate planning to how I would reflect on and learn from the results of my decisions. As a result, Intentionality is baked into the 2HLL model to support your Why.

This doesn't mean everything went according to plan for me! The first year was very hard, and I think it is important to be transparent about that. I'd never owned a business before. I didn't close every single client starting on Day 1. I felt uncomfortable implementing new processes and procedures. I had to learn the law. Some marketing efforts bore fruit, but others were a waste of time and money (I prefer the term "data gathering opportunity"). My presentations had technological glitches and mistakes. I was so nervous to give a commercial at my weekly Business Network International (BNI) networking event that I almost quit. On more than one occasion, I came home, shut the door behind me, and simply burst into tears.

Being committed to an intention to support my autonomy, connectedness, and competence does mean I was able to gauge each result against a clear vision and adjust accordingly. This ability to Iterate (another 2HLL value) with minimal judgment and recriminations is the foundation of my success and a core element of the 2HLL program. Although I was committed to excellence in the estate plans I created, I was not a perfectionist about the business side of my practice. That was a place where I experimented, even played, with opportunities and possibilities, both inside and outside the legal community.

Other 2HLLs have embraced experimentation too, with our full support. It's not our way or the highway. There is no one "right" way to practice estate planning law, just like there is no one right way to practice medicine, to be a personal trainer, or to run a nail salon. Sarah adjusted her pricing model based on her region of the country and found she closed more clients. Another 2HLL, who had an established estate planning practice, runs a hybrid model, serving some clients virtually while acknowledging that referrals from seniors may require more face-to-face meetings and paper documents. Again, 2HLL is focused on what works for **you**.

Is It Really Okay to Do This?

If you're feeling some internal pushback from the voices — social media or otherwise — telling you what a "good lawyer" does, I hear you (and so did Lenore). However, if you've picked up this book, chances are that you're already unhappy or dissatisfied with your current circumstances. Another "reality" is that words like "good" or "successful" somehow manage to be both slippery concepts to pin down and consist of right angles that human lives rarely fit neatly into. **Rather than living in the current of someone else's definition of "good" or "success" — financial, material, emotional — I argue that it's more rewarding to know your own Why and to live Intentionally.** Life does not give you an A+, ever, but it really doesn't hand out high grades for succeeding if your success is defined by someone else. The realization that you're failing at achieving someone else's vision is a very, very bitter pill to swallow.

Once Lenore got clear on her values, she felt far less interested in whatever the social media algorithms were serving up. Less time on social media meant she felt better about following her own path, which created a virtuous circle with her 2HLL implementation efforts. It turns out that her Reality didn't need to be anything like a Reel. It just needed to be hers.

How 2HLL Members Envision Success

I asked 2HLLs to share their own visions of success and what their ideal lifestyle would look like. Here are some of the responses:

- "I think success initially looks different to me than it might a few years from now. **Right now, success to me is being able to pay off my debt and keep up with my current expenses, both personal and business-related. It does not mean me creating a million-dollar law firm or hiring other attorneys or even paralegals in a brick-and-mortar office space. ...** I want to take as many clients as I can without sacrificing that flexibility and quality time with my family but while still being able to save for the future."
- "To me, success is more than just professional achievements; it's about the positive impact I can have on people's lives. **Success also includes the flexibility to immerse myself in the things I love, be it spending quality time with loved ones, pursuing personal passions, or contributing to my community**. Ultimately, I want to create a harmonious balance between my professional fulfillment and a rich personal life."
- **"Success is being able to do the things I want to do. Having the time and money to support my family and create the life I want."**
- "Success is achieving my 5, 10, 15, and 20 year goals I have set out for my firm. **I want to grow my firm to be one of the prominent ones in our state**. My ideal lifestyle is to work when and wherever I want."
- "I define success as having a fulfilling career that allows me to spend guilt-free time with my family. **The estate planning practice I built using the 2HLL methodology has empowered me to create a business I love and be a present parent to my kids.**"

- **"Success means freedom — Freedom of time, money, and purpose**. Ideally, I would like to be flexible and travel while helping clients from anywhere in the world."
- **"I want to provide a comfortable life for my family while also spending as much time with them as possible**. I want to be able to do work that matters and that helps people. I want my son to remember that I was always there for him and that he always had what he needed."
- **"For me, success is setting your own schedule, having happy clients (mostly), and being able to pay my bills and enjoy life."**
- **"To me, success can be measured in how much time-freedom I have.** Work is and probably will always be a really significant part of my life, but doing that work on my terms is so important. **My ideal lifestyle is one where I have a lot of interests outside of work and I have the time to pursue them without constantly feeling guilty because I 'should' be working more on the million-dollar law practice I 'should' want to build**."
- **"To me, success is complete freedom over my time and my schedule. It means being my boss and not having to ask permission to take the morning off to chaperone my child's field trip or to take multiple vacations a year**. It especially means freedom to spend time with my kids; not just be physically with them, but actually be mentally present and not distracted by work calls and emails and work demands that require my immediate attention."
- "Success will be **doing what I want and when I want without anything in my business slowing down**. Whether there are others handling tasks or things happening by automation, everything will keep going when I'm not there. And **when I am working with clients, they are the clients I want and I am**

providing the experiences and impact in their lives I seek to give them."

There are common threads to the definitions of success people bring to 2HLL: **time freedom, a salary that provides for a family, meaningful work, and independence. In other words, 2HLLs value autonomy, impact, and connection in all the forms they manifest in their lives.** Those are the qualities people join 2HLL to develop and refine in their practices — a proven and tested model to live a life you love without leaving the law.

If these definitions of success resonate with you more than the traditional lawyer definitions that include making partner, wearing busyness and exhaustion like a badge of honor, charging a high billable hour rate, and constant conflict, 2HLL is the program for you.

Passion Has a Place

You all know by now I have a passion for ballet (remember my dream of dancing the Dew Drop Fairy in *The Nutcracker*?!) How does my passion for ballet show up in my current life? Living in New York City is a very good start! I am able to attend multiple performances of my favorite company, the New York City Ballet, at Lincoln Center every year. I watch up-and-coming dancers perform, noting their progression from the nearby School of American Ballet to the Corps to Soloist to Principal Dancer. I interact with the dancers and community in person and on social media. I volunteer and attend events and workshops. I am able to do these things because I have total control over my schedule. A Wednesday afternoon dress rehearsal of Swan Lake? Sign me up! There are few places I would rather be.

Your passions can weave into your life in many ways ... if you build a career that offers you the autonomy — time and financial resources — to enjoy them.

EXERCISE:

1. Keeping in mind your Why and your current obligations, how do you define success?
2. Which intentions (processes you can commit to) feel they would move you towards living your Why more fully?
3. What do you need to do to start moving towards that feeling and away from your current Reality? What would give you more of a sense of meaning?
4. Who can support you in more fully living into intentions that move you towards the success that matters to you?
5. What can you remove from your life that will give you space for something new to flourish?

In the next chapter, I'll identify the day-to-day support structure to move forward toward your Why and your definition of success. I'll look at how identifying and aligning with your values reduces the helplessness associated with "little t" trauma.

Chapter Summary

- Great news! The 2HLL focuses on your reality, not social media.
- Once you know your Why, it's time to get real and define what success means to you.
- You don't have to be passionate about your practice area or the law for your work to feel intrinsically motivating or meaningful.
- Focusing on your own definition of success and intentionally working toward more autonomy, impact, and connection reduces "little t" trauma.
- Make sure the ladder you're climbing is leaning against your own wall, not someone else's.

Visit lifestylelawyerrevolution.com for free resources!

Three
Values Matter

When your values are clear to you, making decisions becomes easier.
— Roy E. Disney

Living to our values means that we do more than profess our values; we practice them. We walk our talk — we are clear about what we believe and hold important, and we take care that our intentions, words, thoughts, and behaviors align with those beliefs.
— Brene Brown

When she was considering leaving her Big Law job, Sarah's inner critic was relentless, loud, and vocal in telling her what a screw-up she was. She wasn't living in alignment with her own values, but other associates from her hiring year were surviving, even thriving, in the same atmosphere that was breaking her down. Obviously, her inner critic said, the fault lay with her: she wasn't good enough, strong enough, competitive enough, political enough, or smart enough to have chosen a different path when she graduated! Law school was a mistake, and so was the Big Law job she coveted and competed to win. She'd invested several years on the path towards partnership, and that was time wasted.

Hey!* her inner critic shouted. *If you leave Big Law, you're a failure who quits when things get tough, and you have to admit to everyone that you made a big mistake!

Let's not even get into what your Inner Critic may be saying if you weren't destined for Big Law, didn't land at the top of your class, or didn't make Law Review. From the application process through the competition to make partner, practicing law offers many opportunities for your Inner Critic to get up on a soapbox and start shouting.

Why do some first-year associates thrive at Big Law firms? How do some family law practitioners last for several decades of court appearances, contentious opposing counsel, and emotionally demanding clients, whereas others can only endure a few years, even months? The answer to this question doesn't lie in knowing your Why. And it's only partially answered by knowing your vision of success. The true answer lies underneath both your Why and your vision of Success. **The answer lies in your values.**

Values 101

Oxford Languages defines values as "a person's principles or standards of behavior; one's judgment of what is important in life." These are not hard and fast laws like gravity. They vary from person to person, family to family, and culture to culture.

Think of values as existing in a ratio. Sarah valued competitiveness and hard work. She also valued time with family and friends, a more relaxed lifestyle, and the freedom to set her own schedule. Her fellow associates at her Big Law firm also likely valued family time, relaxation, and freedom. **The distinction lies in the ratio or proportionality**. Sarah valued her time and her freedom more than she valued the competitiveness and long hours necessary to make partner. Getting clarity around her values made it possible for her to more confidently step away from Big Law and into a solo EP practice.

Let's be clear: no one is wrong here.

You can aspire to get in as many hours as humanly possible fishing from a secondhand row boat while still paying the bills and be just as successful as someone who aspires to "the 1 percent" levels of wealth and possessions and dreams of posing next to their Bugatti for millions of adoring social media followers. A Big Law associate working 15-hour days does not care less for their family than someone working 8 a.m. to 5 p.m. and taking a lunch break to volunteer at their kids' school. **There are no wrong answers here, only layers of answers that will shift and change as you live. Your answer merely needs to be yours**. I call this being congruent, meaning that your moment-to-moment decisions are in harmony or agreement with your true self, your values, and your character.

Sounds great. But what about that Reality you talked about?

Fair point. I think it's only right to say that very few people live congruent lives every moment of the day. Many people may feel that they're living incongruently, and their circumstances preclude them from regaining alignment. Bills have to be paid. Children have to be clothed, fed, educated, nurtured. Homes, cars, and possessions require maintenance. That sense of wading through the molasses of Reality is real.

It's important to note that it's very easy to drift from our values, often unconsciously, through little concessions — "I'll work late tonight" becomes "I work late every night." "I only answer urgent client emails nights and weekends" becomes "Excellent customer service means I answer client emails within two hours 24/7/365." Incrementally, you drift away from your value of time with family because you're missing dinner five nights out of seven or your value of being present when playing basketball with your kids because you're constantly checking email. When it comes to time management and personal and professional boundaries, we are all always at the top of a steep and slippery slope.

When you're incongruent with what you believe to be meaningful and worthy — what you feel is important in life — you start to feel off. Initially, this manifests in an internal feeling that's like a grain of sand in your sock. It's mildly irritating, maybe distracting, but you can probably keep on walking. But when a small pebble joins the first, or you pick up a burr right next to your ankle bone, you end up with a sore spot that becomes a blister, then an open wound.

What's also real is that you can live more congruently, with more autonomy, impact, and connection.

The 2HLL Values

All courses, programs, and workplaces come with a set of values built into them. We've already mentioned Intentionality. Let's go through a few more of ours.

2HLL's model is built on the value of **Education**. From the initial marketing efforts through to the signing ceremony, 2HLL-trained lawyers are constantly educating. This is necessary to generate business because most of our clients don't really know why they are hiring us (and therefore resist writing the check.) And they won't know why they should hire us without our help. It's not like this in all areas of law, by the way. When you call a personal injury attorney after being rear-ended, for example, you know exactly why you are calling. You understand the problem (an injured back) and the solution (hiring a lawyer). Who do I make the check out to?

It's not like that with estate planning. People don't know the problem (state intestacy laws) and the solution (hiring an attorney to create a plan that overrides the state intestacy laws). It's why I provide a seminar/webinar framework, including slides and talking points that focus on educating your community and prospective clients that they have an injured back and just don't know it.

Education takes place in the context of another core value: **Relationship.** I provide a sales framework that focuses on education and good old-fashioned human connection — whether in person or via Zoom — to support every step in the client acquisition process, from gathering leads to signing the engagement letter. My networking strategies focus on building and leveraging relationships with other professionals in your community, including financial advisors, life insurance agents, and CPAs. No hard sell tactics. Just educating, using facts in the context of building and nurturing the relationship.

The third guiding principle for 2HLL is **Iteration**. Although the foundational 2HLL course provides everything you need to set up and grow your estate planning practice, it would be magical thinking for me to claim, and you to believe, that buying the course will solve all your problems straight away. Although my members see an ROI (return on investment) from their investment in 2HLL with two or three estate planning clients, and their investments in technology paid back each year with the first client of the year, the ones with the most ongoing success relaxed their value of Perfection and opened to Iteration. It's not enough to just subscribe to the workout app. You have to actually do the pushups if you want to see results. And we can't do the pushups for you.

In fact, 2HLL members find that the more they're willing to experiment and iterate, i.e., the more "entrepreneurial" they are, the faster their business grows. This might include hiring a virtual assistant (VA), hosting webinars even though you're nervous, or learning how to build relationships with potential clients in the Peace of Mind Planning Session™. **When you look at the process as iterative rather than a win/lose or A+/F graded process, you can relax into the process, experiment, and find what works for you and the community you serve.**

This single mindset shift from perfection to Iteration has a profound impact on everything from your work life and professional relationships to your home life and your inner world. Shift your perfectionism into the back seat with your inner critic and watch your mental and emotional health start to thrive. They're going to get along great back there anyway.

My Values

Where did the values of Education, Relationship, and Iteration come from? Directly from my own values. **My top priority is to build relationships and share knowledge so others succeed**. My other top values include:

Independence
Respect
Transparency
Optimism
Grit
Sincerity
Inclusion
Diversity
Community
Value

When I talk to prospective members in 2HLL discovery calls, I often point out that Opportunity, Inclusion, Diversity, and Community create a tide that lifts more than the student's ship. A 2HLL student's success provides for their family; it also provides an opportunity for the student to serve their community in a deeply meaningful way, and to provide feelings of security for their clients. **My vision of success does not include me being on top of a pyramid, gaining all the money and accolades**. I want to share my wealth of education and experience with others so you, too, can grow as lawyers and entrepreneurs and then, as you are able, pay it forward. I know you will.

How Did I Overcome All Those Zeroes?

Finally, let's touch on Grit because it's an essential value for 2HLL. Remember my love of ballet? My mother, divorced and working to support her three daughters, couldn't afford the classes. That meant I worked from the time I was 12 years old to pay for my own ballet classes and costumes and to fund my summer dance programs in Seattle and Aspen. I started by delivering the *Des Moines Register*. For the record, at that time, the *Des Moines Register* was delivered in the mornings, seven days a week. A single Sunday paper was 2–3 inches thick, and I was under 5 feet tall. I got up at 4:30 a.m., before school, to assemble, carry, and distribute papers until I was old enough to graduate to shifts at Long John Silvers.

If both of those jobs sound physically taxing and uninteresting, it's because they were. Delivering newspapers in Iowa summers and winters, or standing over fryers and handing out malt vinegar sauce packets, was bearable because I loved ballet, and the only way I would be able to study dance was to work. So I showed up, morning after morning, shift after shift, sick or healthy, tired or rested, stressed about school or not.

That's Grit.

Surely, starting The Law Office of Laura Cowan was easier than that? No, it wasn't. I started in the pre-pandemic era, toting my slide projector and business cards around Manhattan on the subway, going to weekly 7 a.m. networking meetings, meeting with people for lunch and coffee, writing checks bigger than I'd ever written in my life, crossing my fingers someone would hire me so I could pay the rent. When members join 2HLL feeling stressed about the costs and their revenue stream, I know exactly how they feel. When I hung out my shingle, I knew I provided a service I believed in. I joined communities of like-minded people to gain knowledge and support and built relationships with fellow lawyers, entrepreneurs, and clients. I invested heavily in courses and coaching, ultimately spending over $150,000 on programs both in and outside the legal community. And then, I did the hard work of implementing those programs (i.e., I did the pushups.) And I leveled up on all of this — education, relationship, and iteration — when I started 2HLL to teach other people how to do what I've done.

YOUR VALUES

The following exercise will help you start thinking about your values and where you might be out of alignment. Just as it's easier to not step on the scale and face the fact that our pants don't fit for a reason, it's easier to not think about how adrift we are ... and yet it must be done. Identifying ways in which the work you're already doing aligns with your values automatically reduces the "little t" trauma of helplessness.

EXERCISE:

My members' survey responses offering their definitions of success revealed something of their values; **if success meant enough money and freedom to create and enjoy a comfortable life, then our members value freedom, a steady income, and flexibility**.

1. Return to your vision of success. What does that vision indicate that you value?
2. Does that feel congruent with who you are and your roles in life?
3. How can you move closer to what you feel is of utmost importance?

If you haven't thought about your values in a while, we've got you. **Visit lifestylelawyerrevolution.com for an exercise designed to help you identify your values.**

2HLL Members' Values

What do 2HLL members say about their values, and how do they bring them to bear in their practices?

- "Hard work, commitment, resilience, spirituality, simplicity. **I try to make a conscious effort to check myself and [bring] myself back to alignment when I slip.**"
- "My values include doing good for others, loving my neighbors as myself and living a godly life. **I am in alignment with my values and each day that I can help someone and support my family my life has meaning.**"
- "My current values center around **integrity, compassion, and a commitment to continuous growth.** I believe in fostering genuine connections with others, both personally and professionally, and strive to approach challenges with resilience and empathy. I can confidently say that I am making conscious efforts to integrate my values into various aspects of my life. **Leaving my full-time corporate lawyer job recently and starting my own legal practice is a critical step to ensure that my work aligns with a sense of purpose and contributes positively to those in my community.** I believe that my life is meaningful. **While challenges and uncertainties are inevitable, now my life has a clearly defined purpose.**"
- "Am I finding joy in what I'm spending my time on every day? Am I doing what I want to do? Am I feeling like I'm spending plenty of time with my family? Do I feel good about the work I'm doing? Am I taking care of my mind, body and soul? I am living more in alignment now with these values than I ever have. **So**

many good changes in my life have occurred during the time that I've been taking this course."

- "For the longest time I was not in alignment with my values. [My previous role] did not fit in with the idea of helping others and being of service. In this role as an EP attorney, I am so excited to share the knowledge I have gained over the last few months to help others. I love knowing that what I do can help someone find some peace for their life now as well as once they die. **I still feel I have one foot in and one foot outside of my values, but as each day passes, I am closer and closer to living the best version of my life!**"
- "[Peace – kindness – growth – security – authenticity. **It's always going to be a work in progress, but I am much more aligned with these than I was a few months ago, before starting 2HLL**. As I try to shape my law practice into what I want it to be, I find myself reflecting on these values as I make decisions."
- **"Not selling my clients estate planning packages they don't need is my primary business value**. Creating rapport, ensuring my clients feel they received great service for their money, and building my business slowly but steadily at a rate I can handle."
- "My current values are service to my clients and staying true to myself. I don't always meet my own expectations but I have a lot of goals and sometimes have to stretch to get there. **I feel more fulfilled now than I did for many years because I'm building something of my own from the ground up**."

Finally, values don't have to be cerebral and ethereal. One 2HLL responded this way:

- "Be prepared and don't be a jackass. My family is of utmost importance. Mostly I live in alignment with [my values]."

Don't be a jackass. (Really, is there any value more important than that?)

PART ONE CAPSTONE EXERCISE:

You've explored your Why, your vision of success, and your top values. Let's bring it all together. Remember, you look back not to judge but rather to learn then make a plan.

On a clean sheet of paper or in a new document:

1. Bring together your Why, your vision of success, and your top values.
2. What surfaces as you look at these? Pay careful attention to any feelings that surface.
3. What possibilities come to mind to move you into congruence and reduce that sense of helplessness? Again, pay attention to the feelings that surface.

Revisit this exercise several times over the next few weeks. Do your answers still hold true? If not, what's changed, and why?

What about Sarah, who we've been following through the Part One process? When she contemplated leaving her Big Law job, her inner critic called her a failure who makes mistakes and then quits when things get tough.

Sarah wasn't a quitter, and — if you're unhappy at work — neither are you. Winning a game you don't want to play leaves the victory, your character, and your life hollow and less meaningful than it could be. It's smart, savvy, and self-aware to leave work that's not rewarding and try something else.

Sarah's Why: to make Big Law money without the Big Law hours.

Sarah's vision of success: A thriving solo estate planning practice contained to a 9-5 weekday schedule, allowing her time to serve on various philanthropic boards in her community and enjoy time with her friends.

Sarah's values: Independence, Community, Service.

Adam's Why: to maximize the amount of time he spent with his teenage children before they left home.

Adam's vision of success: transition to an estate planning practice without losing the income he'd built up in his family law practice to free up the time and energy pouring into the court schedule and his demanding clients' needs.

Adam's values: Family, Providing, Independence.

You've now finished Part One of this book: taking stock of where you are. In Part Two, I'll demonstrate the specific elements of 2HLL — **how shifting to the entrepreneurial lawyer mindset changes everything, how flat-fee models completely change the attorney/client relationship, and how leveraging technology and a strong team helps you make more money and buy back your time** — and how they come together to support you as you reduce the "little t" trauma in your current practice and live more fully into a congruent, meaningful life.

Let us show you why 2HLL is the way forward!

Chapter Summary

- It's possible to live in harmony with your values as a human being and as a lawyer.
- Doing so leads to you providing value to your clients, which reduces your sense of helplessness.
- Values are the anchors in our day-to-day actions and decision-making processes.
- When your values are in alignment, your decisions move you forward to YOUR success, which supports YOUR why.

Visit www.LifestyleLawyerRevolution.com for more information on the 2-Hour Lifestyle Lawyer Signature Course!

Part Two

How 2HLL Transforms Your Law Practice — and You

Four
The Power of Entrepreneurship via 2HLL, aka Find Your Forward

Life is like the monkey bars: you have to let go to move forward. Once you make the decision to leap into entrepreneurship, be sure to loosen your grasp on old concepts so you can swing your way to new ones.
— Leah Busque (American entrepreneur)

Trust only movement. Life happens at the level of events, not of words. Trust movement.
— Alfred Adler

Anyone who has ever started colts knows this — you cannot teach them anything (stop, go, turn) until they are moving freely forward. Free and forward movement is the basis of all training.
— Julie Goodnight

Wait, What? Horses?

Stick with me on this one. I've mentioned that one of the events in my life that spurred me to start my own estate planning firm was my mother's unexpected death in 2015. Our Lead Mindset Coach, Margaret, who is also my older sister, was equally devastated by our mother's death. While I got busy conquering the world of estate planning in Manhattan, Margaret took a different tack. She fulfilled a childhood dream and bought a horse.

Learning to ride as an adult provided many learning experiences (some of them humiliating, painful, or both), but the one that stuck with Margaret and is applicable to 2HLL is Julie Goodnight's quote above: **you can't improve a horse's performance if the horse is standing still. You need movement.**

This is also true for humans. Working for someone else pays the bills, but it can be a limitation on your forward movement, aka your development and flourishing in the world. You are supporting someone else's vision of success. Some lawyers are fortunate enough to work for someone who gives them free rein, but most are not. Embracing entrepreneurship is a critical component of the 2HLL model because, as author Neale Donald Walsch says, "Life begins at the edge of our comfort zone."

Reality again: being your own boss is a radical change for many people and, frankly, nerve-wracking. I'll talk later about how 2HLL sets you up for success through a comprehensive course and ongoing coaching and also teaches you to use technology and team to gain momentum, but **first, I want to offer that hanging out your own shingle and being your own boss (something people often find so challenging it hinders their forward movement) is actually empowering.**

First, and most obviously, things that live at the edge of our comfort zones and scare us just a bit are often the things that empower us when we tackle them. The habit of avoiding those edges slowly but surely contracts your sense of self until you're living in a box of your own making.

Second, never underestimate the satisfaction that comes with being your own boss and not having to rely on someone else for a paycheck. **The day someone wrote me my first $4,000 check to create their estate plan, I knew my life would never be the same.**

My first client hired me on April 7, 2017. I carefully noted the date on the calendar; it was that profound. It was the first time someone paid me to build my own business and not someone else's. It was the first time I realized I no longer had to rely on someone else to give me a job to support myself or fulfill my professional or personal goals. It was the first time I realized I had potential far greater than what I'd given myself credit for. Getting that first client is life-changing, which is why I celebrate it in 2HLL. Yes, going from homeless to a million-dollar law firm in less than a year is nice (if not realistic) ... but so is selling your first estate plan after 10 years of raising a family or 20 years working for someone else.

Why Entrepreneurship?

What values does being an entrepreneurial attorney support? Let's consider some examples and 2HLL real-world experiences:

1. **Independence: You can work from anywhere in the world, using technologies that became the norm during the pandemic.** My 2HLL member, Maria, is able to work from her home base in the U.S. and from her family's home in Europe on her frequent trips to visit. Another member only hosts client meetings on Tuesdays and Wednesdays. Yet another works 9 a.m. to 2 p.m. each day, then slaps shut his laptop so he can pick up his kids from school. Yet another is running her Midwest law from Portugal, where she recently relocated with her husband

and children. Other members are later in their careers and establishing retirement income options; our younger lawyers who came of age in a digital era want to take advantage of all that a virtual business offers. Everyone finds the flexibility that comes with being your own boss appealing. Finally, 2HLL members who work in litigation-driven practices are actively searching for practice areas that don't require aligning their schedule with the court's schedule.

2. **Control: You can dial up the entrepreneurial side while dialing down the more tedious aspects of a lawyer's life, like scheduling, marketing, and even drafting.** (I'll talk more about this in the upcoming chapters 6 and 7 on Technology and Team.) If, when you completed the What's Your Why exercise, you've found that being a lawyer isn't as appealing as it used to be, but it's also your primary skill set and main source of income for yourself and your family, pivoting to a practice area that allows you to engage with the **business** side of things while utilizing a team to support the **legal** side of things may give you the space, intellectual stimulation, and energy you need to make peace with the law, and maybe love your life again.
3. **Opportunity:** I'll cover in the next chapter how letting go of the billable hour model supercharges your income potential. Once you figure out which marketing techniques and channels provide the steadiest revenue streams, you're able to branch out into other businesses. You could add a complementary practice area like business law to your practice, or you could start a completely different business altogether. One of our members owns a restaurant and a cleaning service in addition to their EP practice. Another has her own fashion design business. Others have found that providing drafting services for other attorneys best suits their personality. Another 2HLL with a background in graphic design develops websites and other services for the

legal community. **Seeing yourself as an entrepreneur shifts your mindset from time and energy as a limited resource (there are only 24 hours in a day) to seeing opportunities everywhere.**

These examples highlight the creativity in entrepreneurship. When you get comfortable doing estate planning presentations, you start to realize the power of standing at the front of the room. What other talks can you give that showcase you as an expert or thought leader in your community? What else are you interested in? Maybe you could join a panel with your newfound confidence. Maybe you could lead a group. When you step outside the box, yes, you lose the floor — the safety net of a salary — but there are also no more walls keeping you trapped.

You've heard me speak a lot about hosting workshops — estate planning seminars and webinars — in your community. **I want to address the elephant in the room: the fear of public speaking.** Most of us hate it. I know I did. Not only that, I was terrible at it, which made me hate it even more! It bothered me so much that, in college, when they handed out the syllabus on the first day of class (yes, this was back in the day when we got a paper syllabus!), the first thing I did was look to see if there was a presentation. And if there was, my day was ruined. Can you relate? I didn't get good at public speaking until I opened my law firm 15 years later and realized it was the best way for me to get estate planning clients. I joined a BNI networking group where you present a commercial every week to dozens of other professionals and started hosting as many in-person workshops as possible. And you know what? I actually started to enjoy public speaking. I am now more excited than nervous about the prospect of speaking in public.

I tell you this because I want you to know it's something you can overcome. Whatever path you choose in life, you will have more impact, influence, and income if you are able to speak in front of others. 2HLL is here to support you in that capacity.

But I'm Not Comfortable Selling Myself!

Being an entrepreneur comes with one very specific perceived negative: attracting people to your business. One of the most common statements I hear when people join 2HLL is some version of this:

I hate marketing. Selling myself does not come naturally to me.

Time for one of the most powerful tools in your Mindset kit, the good old cognitive reframe. With respect, I disagree with the foundation of that statement.

You are not selling *yourself*. You are selling an *outcome*.

I want to repeat that because it's important. You are not selling yourself to your clients. You are selling an outcome that is more aligned with what your client wants and less aligned with your state's default rules of intestacy. Yes, we create documents. But the documents merely memorialize the desired outcome. People may say, "I want a will," but what they really mean is, "I want to make sure my sister gets custody of my minor children should something happen to me." They may say, "I want a trust," but what they really mean is, "I want my affairs to be totally private when I'm gone." They are buying the outcome, and that's what you should be selling.

I firmly believe that estate planning provides a real, vital, and valuable opportunity to perform the counselor role of being an attorney. Very few people are comfortable thinking about death, let alone their own death. Parents don't want to think about what happens if they die, leaving behind young children to be raised, or if their young adult is in an accident. Grown children struggle with the reality of losing a parent; a conversation made even more difficult if the parent struggles to face their own demise. Conversations about property and assets can exacerbate divisions in families. These are hard conversations to have. With practice, you can counsel clients in more ways than the traditional lawyer title implies. **Make no mistake, you want to get good at this because this is what will set you apart from Legal Zoom and AI.**

No matter how advanced technology gets, people will always want the connection — and outcome — that comes from hiring a lawyer.

When you get comfortable with hard conversations and counseling, you increase your likelihood of connecting with clients as human beings, which increases your chances of five-star reviews and referrals. Never forget that people hire you because of the way you make them FEEL — not for drafting the perfect Rule Against Perpetuities clause.

Counseling your clients so they understand how an estate plan makes those difficult moments in the hospital or at the funeral home easier for their loved ones goes a long, long way toward providing the peace of mind we all want. **Your expertise and "bedside manner" in solving that very complex and personal problem is what you're marketing.**

Collecting stories to demonstrate the consequences of a poorly planned estate transition also helps with marketing. Margaret speaks from personal experience with this. When our mother died, Margaret served as the executor of the estate. However, our mother's will was created by a software package and had not been properly executed. It also was a will, not a fully funded revocable living trust, which meant the estate had to go through probate. The consequences? The process took longer and cost far more than hiring an estate planning attorney to prepare a living trust or a properly executed will would have cost — a result our frugal mother would not have wanted.

When Margaret finished that process, she and her husband promptly hired an estate planning attorney to ensure their assets went into a trust, guardians were named for their minor child, and their wishes about distributing assets as that child attained majority were clearly laid out. Margaret knew from painful personal experience that this was a kindness to the people who would be left behind — their son and their siblings — if the unthinkable happened.

2HLL's Robust Models Make It Easy To Build Your Estate Planning Practice

The 2HLL is based on two models. The first is the overall 2HLL business model: **Attract, Close, Execute (ACE)**. The second is the "how" of that model: **Principled Relational Sales (PRS)**.

My **Attract, Close, Execute (ACE)** model provides a step-by-step plan for how to work with each individual client's assets and relationships in a single meeting that significantly improves your confidence and your likelihood of closing at the fee you deserve. I teach you how to shift the focus to the revenue-generating aspects of the model — Attracting and Closing — and away from administrative tasks and data entry. This is the more tedious element of the work and is also of the least financial value to you, the attorney. My **Principled Relational Sales (PRS)** model teaches you the soft skills necessary to have a relationship-building conversation with clients that goes beyond the work product — where the relationship you're building far exceeds anything AI can offer.

The truth is, your work could save clients thousands or even millions of dollars in probate costs or estate taxes while ensuring their wishes are followed, their dependents are taken care of, and the entire family's privacy remains intact. **Clearly and confidently demonstrating to the client the value of choosing to work with an attorney on their estate plan rather than letting the state — or AI, a financial advisor, or some online form — do it for them ensures your fee is well worth the investment.**

I developed and tested both the ACE and the PRS methods as I grew my practice. Almost 500 lawyers have implemented them in their own law firms. In the course and during coaching sessions, I break the process down into separate components and teach you how to refer back to them again and again as your business grows, which makes it easy to learn and implement them. Together, they provide a solid foundation for your estate planning business.

EXERCISE:

Keeping in mind that your goal is to educate your contacts and community about the need for an estate plan and your services in providing them, take a moment to brainstorm potential opportunities:

1. Who do you know?
2. What groups do you belong to or participate in?
3. What industry connections do you or close contacts have? One 2HLL spoke to a national industry group and gathered multiple hot leads for her state and others to refer out to the 2HLL community.
4. Are there places — retreat centers, yoga studios, and so on — where you can offer workshops, talks, or seminars?

Once you get good at converting attendees to paying clients, you have a process that works and can now start putting money into ads.

What Problem Do You Want to Have?

If you've never tried, how will you ever know if there's any chance?
— Jack Ma

When you decide to quit that Big Law job, leave the corporate world, or add a new practice area to your current business, it's easy to have a Pollyanna attitude that everything will be easy, fun, and so much better than things are now.

They won't ... unless you take small, intentional, measurable steps at the very edge of your comfort zone. This is where the Grit value really applies.

Here's another cognitive reframe: **reducing your sense of "little t" trauma as a lawyer depends on you deciding what problem you want to have**.

Big Law jobs come with Big Law salaries and the chance to work with people considered to be "the best of the best" (if you use law school prestige and class rankings as a gauge of someone's capability or worth — we don't). They also come with Big Law firm problems. Do you want the night, weekend, and holiday workload, as well as the politics and competitiveness of the partner position? Do you want the travel, the trial schedule, or the socializing that goes into rainmaking?

Hanging out your own shingle comes with some of the same problems — nights, weekends, and holidays lost to work. You may be beholden to a court's trial schedule. You may still work nights, weekends, and holidays. You won't face competition for a partner position, but you will face (hopefully friendly) competition from other attorneys within your community, as well as personnel issues like hiring the right paralegal or virtual assistant. You'll still have to make it rain. Yes, I'll go to a *Swan*

Lake dress rehearsal at 1 p.m. on a Wednesday ... but I'll likely work Friday to make it up.

Being a lawyer-entrepreneur means you're choosing a different set of problems. However, your problems are much more likely to be within your control to resolve, which reduces that sense of helplessness. If the assistant isn't working out, you decide how to approach that problem and implement the solution. If your schedule is too full (a great problem to have!), you decide whether to refer the business out or hire a paralegal or junior attorney. If you don't have enough business, you turn to the Iterate value and tweak your marketing and networking strategies. If your processes aren't working, you research technology solutions and choose one.

EXERCISE:

Which set of problems would you rather have? Reflect on that, and journal about what comes up in the space provided below, or visit lifestylelawyerrevolution.com to access the exercise.

I'll talk more in chapter 6 (Tech) about the 2HLL recommended Tech Stack and how technology can buy back hours — yes, hours — in your day, not to mention your attention span. Until then, think of yourself as a constantly developing human being and lawyer. If you're reading this book, chances are you're already uncomfortable in your current work environment. **Maybe it's time to swap one set of problems for a more exciting, more engaging, and more expansive set of problems for your own dream by becoming a lawyer-entrepreneur.**

2HLL Supports Members in the Entrepreneurial Journey

I asked 2HLL members if they considered themselves to be entrepreneurs, and got back a wide range of responses:

- **"Yes, and have been such before as well in different stages in my life.** It has been harder to implement and carry forward that creative side of myself more in recent years due to mounting other obligations ... to where I felt that I lost my sense of self some. However, the recognition of that allowed me to pursue again my passion and the exercise of my creative side."
- **"At first, I wasn't sure if the entrepreneurial route was for me. However, I think that my creative side allows me to think outside the box."**
- **"I am a born entrepreneur**. I love the independence it brings, I am self-driven and focused, and I don't mind working hard to reap the benefits."
- "I became an entrepreneur when I decided to start my own fashion business. **Entrepreneurship, for me, is not just about the specific business ventures; it's a mindset that thrives on innovation and a proactive approach to seizing opportunities.** The previous entrepreneurial experience compelled me to step outside my comfort zone continually."

- "Yes, I see myself as an entrepreneur. **Running a law office is a business. Nothing gets in the way of that now that I realize how important self-promotion and marketing are.**"
- **"I don't see myself as an entrepreneur yet. Technically I am, I run my own solo law firm, but it doesn't feel like that quite yet.** I'm hoping once I make more of a social media presence, attend more events, and begin webinars this feeling will change."
- "Definitely! **I want to exude boss b*tch energy in all that I do,** including and especially in what makes me money."
- **"Ultimately, yes — because I'm shifting my mindset to view my law practice as a business and not trying to make it fulfill me in a way that it can't.**"
- "I absolutely see myself as an entrepreneur. **I worked for years with founders/entrepreneurs and one thing I learned was confidence and stubbornness are the hallmarks of making a business thrive and succeed.** I am taking those lessons to my own business and feel confident I can make this law firm successful."
- **"No, not right now but I'm hopeful.** ...I think I'll feel more like an entrepreneur as time goes by and I get more comfortable and confident that I can get through the challenges."
- **"I still don't feel like a savvy entrepreneur. But I am certainly one that understands this journey is one of constant growth.** Every obstacle is an opportunity to sharpen a skill or become even more resilient."
- **"Yes I do.** I have now started two businesses, and I am the first generation in my family to have done so. **Time and family responsibilities are getting in the way, and I know they take priority. That is why I need Laura's program.** It was a very worthwhile investment."

- "Yes. **As I am thinking more and more on automation and removing myself from many of the tasks, I see myself as more and more of an entrepreneur.**"
- And mine: **"I didn't become the person I was meant to be until I started business."**

It's Worth It

Life at the edge of your comfort zone isn't, well, comfortable, but the lessons you learn there are life-changing. Margaret no longer owns the horse she bought in those difficult months after our mother died, but her successes and "learning opportunities" (those often painful failures) continue to shape her coaching, her sense of herself and what she can do, and every relationship she's in. The same goes for me. It's 11 a.m. on a Tuesday, and I just texted a friend from an Open House at the School of American Ballet at Lincoln Center in New York City.

11 a.m. on a Tuesday.

Being your own boss opens up opportunities to engage with family, friends, and your interests or passions on your own schedule.

I got to that Open House for one reason: because years earlier, I made the hard choice to go into business for myself. I got in motion and found my forward. Get started! Take action and learn while in motion. You might regret it, but you're going to have regrets anyway.

EXERCISE:

1. What are you curious about regarding 2HLL or your current career?
2. What experiments can you run? How can you iterate on those experiments?
3. How will 2HLL help you achieve your career goals?

What's Next: One comfort zone most lawyers struggle with is the billable hour, and oh, boy, did we hear from our members on that issue. I've got a solution for that in the next chapter.

Chapter Summary

- The mindset shift from being a lawyer to being a lawyer-entrepreneur offers Autonomy, Competence, and Connection. You gain control over your work, your schedule, and your business, reducing the sense of helplessness from "little t" trauma.
- It's not easy to make that shift.
- The 2HLL provides comprehensive models and materials to support you as you do.
- You also need Grit.
- In the end, the payoffs in confidence, freedom, and opportunity are worth the work.

Visit www.LifestyleLawyerRevolution.com for more resources!

Five
Beyond Billable Hours to Value-Based Pricing

How do you feel about billable hours?

I'm going to start with member quotes for this chapter because **no other question I asked generated the same number of emphatic responses with all caps and emotionally charged words.** Here are 2HLL member responses to being asked how they felt about billable hours:

- "Hourly billing is the **bane** of many attorneys, and I am no different."
- "BLEH. It is **terrible** and god awful."
- "I **hated** billable hours because **I felt I had to overwork to count**." (Side note: Ouch. Just ... ouch.)
- "I **hate** billable hours. **Clients hate billable hours**."
- "The billable hour **takes away my incentive to complete tasks efficiently**."
- **"It's the WORST part of being an attorney** ... Not being able to take a vacation without taking into account billing for that time off either before or after. It is time-consuming to enter time and keep track of everything you do."

- "I would **feel guilty** if I thought I should have done something quicker and wondered how long it took others."
- **"Despise billing. Hate, loathe."**
- "Not a fan of billable hours. **It leaves matters very uncertain for clients.**"
- **"Billable hours is a scam."**
- "I don't mind billable hours and the process of billing people. My frustration stems from **chasing people for their remaining retainer ... or chasing people for their bills.**"
- "I think I spent more time inputting my tracked time than I spent on some projects. **Madness!**"
- **"I forget to bill and I cost myself so much money."**

And there you have it.

Many of the 2HLL members I surveyed said they joined 2HLL because they wanted to reclaim time for their families, for their overall mental and physical well-being, or for their hobbies and interests. But they immediately run into a mental speed bump around how they charge for their services and around their identities as lawyers.

The speed bump? The practice of charging by the billable hour, as counted in six-minute increments.

This creates an extraordinarily unhelpful link between your time and the client's money. In order to make more money, you either need to work more hours or you need to bill more per hour, preferably both. This is how Big Law associates end up leaving the office at 2 a.m. to shower and change clothes, then be back by 5 a.m. Somehow, this not only becomes normal but something to be proud of.

Think back to your revised vision of success. If that work schedule appeals to you, if you love your job and the rewards it's bringing, I fully support that! Again, I'm not here to define success for you. But, if that kind of work-life balance has burned you out, if it's damaged relationships with people you love and who love you, if it's left you sleep-deprived, with an ulcer and your hair falling out from stress, with no time for rest and the things that nourish you, the 2HLL flat-fee model provides a different option. Let's examine why.

The Billable Hour Model Limits Your Income

Working more and billing at a higher rate is not the most efficient way to increase your income. You will run into a ceiling in both cases. We all have the same number of hours in a day. There is a limit to what your community will pay for your services. While the Mindset training offered in 2HLL focuses on strategies to improve your time management, your energy is also a limited resource subject to burnout. There is a ceiling to how much you can boost your income by working more, smarter, or harder.

The most efficient way to increase your income is to bring in more business. That's why 2HLL teaches the attorney to focus on attracting, educating, and closing clients, which generates revenue, and relying on technology and targeted staffing for the execution part of the model. This helps with "little t" trauma because you shift your focus to what actually influences your income — new business — rather than obsessively focusing on how the hours are spent after you've already signed the client.

Remember my point from the Introduction that lawyers' professional lives involve being exposed to complex, prolonged interpersonal battles, which can lead to the sense of trapped helplessness that defines "little t" trauma? Thinking of billable hours as "This is the way we've always done it so I can't do it any other way" is thinking that indicates that burnout is lurking just around the corner.

EXERCISE:

Take a moment to answer the following questions:

1. How do you feel about your income strategy and your time management?
2. Do you have enough time? Do you enjoy how you spend it at work (and if "enjoy" is too big a leap, try for "I'm okay with it")? Or do you endure the minutes and hours of your professional life?
3. Do you effectively manage your time? Or are you chronically behind the eight-ball, rushing from meeting to client calls to court?
4. Do you wear busyness as a badge of honor? Or does your current workload and schedule contribute to a sense of burnout and desperation?
5. Did you feel like you even had a moment to answer the questions above or the ones woven into earlier chapters?

Let's take a look at the problems stemming from billable hours and the resulting damage it does to the attorney-client relationship.

The Billable Hour Model Damages Relationships

First, I want to acknowledge that litigation matters are different, although retainers are, in essence, a flat fee charged upfront, which is then either refunded because the matter took less time than estimated or added to because the matter took longer than anticipated.

Now let's look at how the billable hour model can damage relationships:

1. Some members point out that **billing by the hour can lead to inefficient work and overworking** because attorneys are not incentivized to work quickly and accurately. This is an insidious mindset issue that may not show up on the surface but rather may be contributing to your "little t" trauma.
2. **Clients experience significant uncertainty** because they do not know how much a work product is going to cost. **It's never a good customer service situation for a client to open a bill and say, "What the actual hell?"** This uncertainty **destabilizes the attorney-client relationship**, which is the source of good reviews and referrals, as well as the source of confidence and trust for both parties.
3. **The billable hour ensures you and your client come to the encounter in an adversarial relationship:** they measure your efforts by your hourly rate without truly understanding the value of the service you provide. Bringing these two things into alignment creates trust, builds the relationship, and leaves you both more confident human beings, rather than the client as an open wallet and the attorney as the pickpocket stealing from it.

4. Most importantly, **under the billable hour, clients do not clearly understand the value of the service they receive and what it's worth to them. They only understand the value of your time when what you really want them to focus on is the outcome, not how long it took you to get there.**

The 2HLL Approach

At 2HLL, we engage with our members from the perspective that you are much, much more than your hourly bill rate. You are a highly educated, experienced professional providing a vital service that saves the client's loved ones time, money, and emotional turmoil. You are charging for your time in law school, your time studying for and sitting for the bar, your experience that allows you to counsel your clients, and your business costs. You are charging for an outcome that can only be provided by a qualified estate planning attorney.

Furthermore, reclaiming your time by extracting yourself from the limiting belief that "billable hours are the only way to go" helps create that sense of spaciousness being an entrepreneur can bring. Meaning, belonging, and contribution come when you're in flow, not when you're tracking, entering, and bickering over hours.

It's worth restating: effectively implementing the ACE (Attract, Close, Execute) and PRS (Principled Relational Sales) models enables you to **clearly and confidently demonstrate to the client the value of hiring you to create their estate plan rather than letting the state — or AI, or a financial advisor, or some online form — do it for them. This ensures that your fee seems well worth the investment.** Quoting your fee becomes much easier when you are able to demonstrate it's going to cost your clients a lot more if they don't hire you than if they do, not only financially but emotionally.

Again, I return to the Education value, which is one of 2HLL's pillars. In essence, 2HLLs charge an up-front flat fee based on what the outcome is worth to the client's family, not how the attorney values their time. Said another way, we charge based on the outcome, not how long it took us to do the work. Clients know what the attorney's services cost. There are no surprises. That's a real benefit to clients and builds the relationship, which is crucial to both parties' satisfaction.

How does the attorney benefit? From the get-go, you take the first and most important step in reclaiming your time. **You separate your sense of self from how much work you can do (which is limited by hours in a day) and build a sense of self as a valued, whole person with education, experience, and a customer-focused orientation. This is valuable insurance against "little t" trauma and burnout.**

Let's see what our members have to say about how they feel after switching to the 2HLL flat-fee model:

- "With the teachings from 2HLL, **I have a clear understanding of the value I bring to my clients and how to effectively communicate and justify that value**."
- "I have always used a flat fee model and felt comfortable with it. **I have increased my fees** and feel more confident charging what I'm worth."
- "[We] didn't know how to quote estate planning fees, and with the lessons from 2HLL, **we were confident we were providing value to our clients**."
- "Absolutely. When I started, I felt anxious, but **now I feel at peace**."
- "I feel better about the fees. At times in the past, I have felt that [my fee] for a trust was too much to ask — even though I knew the time going into trusts. **But now, I am seeing the value of the services I provide**."
- "I think 2HLL has given me some new ways of thinking about the value I provide and some new ways of presenting information to potential clients so they can see the value ... **2HLL has helped**

me confidently quote fees no matter how much the guy across the table/on the Zoom screen thinks it's 'highway robbery.' (Actual client quote.)"

- "I love it. **I just pull up the sheet on the computer and speak very matter of factly about it**. I didn't mind quoting flat fees before, as I did, but now it looks and feels much more professional."
- **"I really benefited from learning how to make my clients see the value in paying for a trust now so as to avoid probate down the road.**"
- "Yes, I feel more confident. I still waiver a bit on my pricing for wills because it feels high. **I remind myself I'd rather [d]o less work for more money and must be comfortable with losing clients who are price shopping**."
- "Yes! **I actually am working a glide path to show value before the fees come up,** but I feel fine about quoting fees because if they don't see our value by the time they speak with us then they aren't the right fit for us and vice versa."
- "As I have really reflected on the time and effort I've put into learning and preparing these things, I've become more comfortable with charging more. **When I first started I was massively undercharging. Now I feel pretty confident**."

The key thing that 2HLL offers, based on the above quotes, isn't only the flat-fee model. That model is not unusual in estate planning, the wider legal community, or the world at large. Can you imagine receiving a bill from your tree service company where the time was calculated in six-minute increments, especially if you weren't home to watch them and make sure they were working efficiently? What stands out to me in the responses is **the growth in our members' confidence to clearly educate prospective clients about the benefits of hiring them in such a way that the value jumps out to the client.**

The best part about a flat-fee model is that you get paid upfront, which incentivizes you to deliver an accurate work product as quickly and cost-effectively as possible so you can serve and support the next client, thereby increasing your earnings.

Working efficiently to serve more clients does not mean that your work is sub-par! There is no logical reason for attorneys to consider themselves exempt from process improvements that benefit them, their clients, and their communities. It simply means you have systems and processes in place that free you up to provide the five-star service your clients deserve. **This mindset shift cannot be overstated. The empowerment that comes from charging what you're worth, automating your workflows, and focusing on building your business is truly life-changing. It happened to me. It's happened for 2HLLs. It can happen to you.**

Chapter Summary

- The world opens up when you shift your mindset from charging clients in minute increments to providing a service for a flat fee.
- Billable hours constrict you and your income potential.
- Many attorneys have a difficult relationship with the billable hour.
- It creates uncertainty for both the lawyer and the client.
- It's not supportive of either your or the client's mental health.
- A flat-fee model ensures you are able to charge what your education and experience are worth while providing superlative value to the client.
- A flat-fee model also supports the kind of relationships that bring in referrals and support your community.
- A flat-fee model frees you up to get more clients, thereby increasing your business.
- Charging a flat fee for your services isn't the only way to reclaim your time and energy and maximize your earning potential. So, next, let's talk tech.

Six
Technology: Your Frenemy

Technology is not your arch-enemy. It is your friend. (Plot twist: it's also your arch-enemy).

I frickin' hate technology.

Andres' path to law school and a legal career didn't follow the traditional path. A talented visual artist and creative with multiple group and solo shows on his CV, Andres realized that he'd have a much stronger position negotiating with gallery owners and production companies if he actually understood the contracts he was paying an agent to read for him. With an established market for his artistic endeavors providing a steady revenue stream, he never intended to work a full-time job as a lawyer because he preferred to align his life with his values of creativity and self-expression.

Reality intervened for Andres when he realized that it had taken him the better part of a week to draft one section of a complex estate plan because his time was so fragmented between the phone ringing, scheduling and rescheduling appointments, answering emails, and meetings with clients where he repeated the same speech, over and over again. **Chronic, "urgent" distractions left him with less time, energy, or attention to focus on the work that, if wrong, could generate a malpractice suit and almost none for his art – what he really valued.**

Technology to the rescue!

The Friend Part of Frenemy: Technology and Time

Before we dig in, I want to make a quick comment about technology and its associated price tag. We do not recommend investing in technology just for the heck of it. Every tool we recommend has been tested by my students and me, which means it is proven to save you time and energy as well as give your clients a better experience. These are investments, not expenses. You may not have to buy each and every one on Day 1, but **the sooner you start treating your practice like a business, the sooner you will start to see how tools like this make more money than they cost**. Let's explore more ways technology can help you reclaim your time and a life you love.

Whether you charge a flat fee or by the billable hour, an attorney's most valuable resource is time. You can always make more money; you cannot get more time. In the last chapter, I talked about the typical attorney relationship with time, and how shifting to a flat-fee model enables you to reclaim your time. **However, your billing structure isn't the only way for you to reclaim your time. Embracing readily available and (often) simple technologies to automate the Execute portion of the ACE model buys back your time so you can put it into your family, friends, or the A and C portions of 2HLL**. Increasing your revenue feels far less daunting and far more possible when you outsource or hire someone to perform the repetitive tasks that don't need a trained lawyer to do them.

I routinely sift through and test possible technology components of a virtual estate planning business and compile an evolving Tech Stack that — with an investment that pays itself back with one closed client — gets you up and running on Day 1. The vetted and tested technologies ensure your work day and the workflows within your practice flow smoothly and efficiently. Who doesn't want more peace of mind at work?

Here are just a few examples of the technologies we recommend implementing[5]:

The Low-Hanging Fruit: Calendly

I asked our members to give us an example of software they've implemented from this stack that made a big difference immediately.

The clear winner in terms of saving time?

Calendly.

Calendly is an appointment booking service that connects to your calendar application, and it allows clients to schedule appointments with you without calling your office. At the time of publication, a Calendly subscription is $10/month for some bells and whistles, and there is a free version that gets you started.

You want to use a service like Calendly. Here's why:

1. **Clients know exactly how much time they're going to spend with you for each meeting.** People like certainty. Offering it creates a sense of relationship and trust. Offering online scheduling software allows people who are "phone-call averse" to book with you without having to speak to you (hint: this includes pretty much everyone born after about 2000 with a special shout-out to the introverts out there, too. We see you but will not call on you!).
2. This reduces the number of demands on your mental energy by creating a framework for scheduling that you can apply in different ways. **Adding the scheduling link to your signature line or creating an automated response that goes to all client emails including scheduling links saves you time and**

5 Recommendations as of publication. We reserve the right to change our recommendations.

mental energy and also empowers your prospective clients to choose the time that works best for them.

3. **You can implement Time Blocking and Time Boxing, two vital and valuable time management techniques, via Calendly.** With Time Boxing, you create boxed-out blocks of time to meet with clients. With Time Blocking, you create blocks of uninterrupted time for things like drafting, staff meetings, or marketing work. Again, creating a sense of control in the chaos goes a long way towards easing that "little t" trauma.
4. With a Calendly subscription, **you can send automated reminders to your booked clients, including links to the relevant intake questionnaire or documents and videos, prior to the meeting**. This also allows you to start setting expectations right away. For example, if the client questionnaire has not been filled out at least 24 hours before the meeting, the meeting will be rescheduled. **You set boundaries, and your prospective clients take some ownership of the process, which builds buy-in and reduces the likelihood they'll go somewhere else.**

Here's what our members had to say about this practice-transforming tool:

- "I'm using Calendly for booking appointments. This is great! **It saves the staff so much time!**"
- "The incorporation of Calendly into my client scheduling process has **saved me numerous back-and-forth emails and phone calls.**"
- "Having a calendaring system to send people my availability has been game changing. **I don't have to waste time and energy emailing back and forth to set times for Zoom meetings with clients.**"

- "Calendly. This was such an amazing program that I didn't realize existed and **love how it's organized my life** and made it easy for clients to schedule with me."

Repetitive Meetings? Loom to the Rescue!

Experienced estate planning attorneys know the struggle is real. Imagine spending hours repeating the same explanations about complex legal documents, day after day, client after client. The back-and-forth of reviewing draft wills and trusts can feel like a never-ending cycle.

Helping clients understand their documents, confirm all names are spelled correctly, and other such details are critical to a quality work product, but it doesn't have to come at the expense of the lawyer's time and energy. Traditional in-person document review meetings, or even a review via Zoom, can be tedious, requiring lawyers to translate complicated legalese into plain English for each client (we all know the frustration of hearing, "What's this Rule Against Perpetuities thing?") This not only eats into time the lawyer should be spending attracting new business and doing legal work, but it can also lead to frustration for clients who might struggle to grasp complex legal concepts on the fly, or who obsess unnecessarily over certain language.

There's a better way! Enter Loom, a video recording tool that can be a game-changer for estate planning attorneys. **By using Loom to create detailed, pre-recorded explanations of the documents, lawyers can free themselves from repetitive live meetings.** By creating a generic video explaining important provisions present in every estate plan, clients can review the information at their own pace, in the comfort of their own homes. A shorter video can be created for explanations specific to each individual client.

Loom videos offer several advantages over traditional meetings.

Clients can pause, rewind, and take notes, ensuring they fully understand each aspect of the document. This empowers them to ask informed questions, if they have them, or simply approve the documents for signature. And the benefits of Loom extend beyond streamlining client communication! You can create training videos for new staff, deliver personalized messages to clients, or even capture video testimonials to showcase your services. Loom is a versatile tool that saves time, improves communication, and ultimately helps build a strong and successful estate planning practice.

Say Goodbye to Repetitive Data Entry with DecisionVault!

We are big fans of DecisionVault at 2HLL. **DecisionVault is a groundbreaking software that streamlines and automates both the intake process and the plan design and drafting process after someone hires you.** It provides estate planning attorneys with a central system for collecting, storing, and integrating client intake information with existing tools. It functions as a portal, allowing multiple sources (you, clients, paralegals, and assistants) to add information at any time.

DecisionVault sets you as the attorney up for success in a way no other software can. Founded by Wouter IJgosse in 2020 for his estate planning attorney wife, Julia, DecisionVault solves the age-old problem of having to retype data over and over again as it moves from client questionnaires to design sheets to drafting software.

First, the intake questionnaire, which is fully customizable, provides a safe, secure way to collect basic information about the prospect's assets, family, and objectives. It's up to you how much information you want to gather before the meeting, but I have found people unwilling to provide even basic information about themselves are almost certainly price-shopping and not a good fit for my firm. For this reason, I require a completed questionnaire before anyone meets with me. DecisionVault also generates reports based on the client questionnaire to assist you at the consultation. This includes an Attorney Matter

Report, excellent for "issue spotting," and an Assets Export that makes calculating estimated probate and estate taxes a breeze.

DecisionVault assists after someone hires you, too. **A fully customizable design sheet is embedded within the software, porting over data from the questionnaire and allowing you to easily document client decisions at the design meeting.** The design sheet then integrates with drafting software like InterActive Legal or WealthDocx, eliminating the need to retype client data yet again. And because it's a portal, DecisionVault sets you up for long-term relationships with your clients whose assets, family, and life will be in constant motion.

We teach DecisionVault in the 2HLL course and have ongoing training so you can use it to its full potential in your practice!

Drafting Software to the Rescue!

Did you know you don't have to cobble together wills and trusts and healthcare proxies from old Word documents passed down from lawyer to lawyer? **There is drafting software to help you easily generate professional, state-specific, and comprehensive estate plans for your clients.** Learning this was what gave me the final burst of confidence I needed to open my own practice! Both InterActive Legal and WealthDocx by WealthCounsel help you quickly and efficiently create an entire suite of estate planning documents. Both also offer education, events, and a community to support your practice!

Drafting software automates many repetitive tasks involved in estate planning document creation. This includes pre-populated templates, built-in clauses, and state-specific variations. Essential documents like wills, trusts, and powers of attorney are generated in a fraction of the time it takes traditional manual drafting. **This frees you up to focus on client service and generating revenue!**

Drafting software also minimizes the risk of errors and inconsistencies that can occur with manual drafting. It helps ensure that documents comply with current laws and regulations, reducing the potential for future issues and protecting your clients' interests. It includes client-friendly features like document summaries that help the client understand the key provisions of their estate plans in clear, layperson's terms. This fosters better communication and informed decision-making throughout the process.

By streamlining workflow and reducing drafting time, estate planning software can boost your overall firm's profitability. You can take on more clients without sacrificing quality or service. It will help you efficiently scale. Finally, utilizing drafting software demonstrates your commitment to efficiency, accuracy, and client education. This can give you a competitive edge in a crowded market, especially for solo or new estate planning lawyers.

Easily Host Webinars with Zoom Webinar

We've spoken a lot about the "A" in ACE — attracting leads! Although there are many ways to get business as an estate planning attorney, including client referrals and networking, **we have found that consistently hosting educational workshops in your community — whether in person or online — is the best way to ensure a consistent flow of warm leads coming through your door.**

That's why we teach our members how to host workshops both in-person and virtually. Although the slides and script may be the same, there are key differences when it comes to running virtual events that I want to highlight. Simply sending out a Zoom link won't cut it — you'll end up with a chaotic event that doesn't lead to conversions. Upgrading to a dedicated webinar platform like Zoom Webinar, Demio, or GoToWebinar can make all the difference. These platforms allow you to create a customized registration page, set up a professional waiting room, and seamlessly incorporate your branding, giving you a polished and conversion-focused presentation.

Second, engagement is key. If people show up and get bored, they are going to leave. You want to do more than just broadcast a presentation. With Zoom Webinar, you can incorporate interactive features that keep your audience engaged. You should be conducting live polls to gauge audience understanding, hosting Q&A sessions, and incorporating handouts in your webinar. These features not only make the event more fun, but they also increase the odds of you moving them down your sales pipeline.

Zoom Webinar seamlessly integrates with your Customer Relationship Management (CRM) software, such as Lawcus or Clio, as well as marketing automation tools like Mailchimp. This allows you to easily capture attendee details during registration (you'll definitely need those emails for follow-up with automated drip campaigns!). Plus, you can use engagement data from the webinar to personalize your follow-up messages, helping to nurture leads and guide them further down your sales funnel.

Fourth, scale is your friend. Zoom Webinar allows you to host workshops for a significantly larger audience compared with regular Zoom meetings. This lets you reach a wider pool of potential clients, maximizing your outreach efforts. **If your practice is virtual, there is no reason you can't promote your events statewide to reach a greater audience!** Furthermore, Zoom Webinar allows you to record your sessions. This recorded content becomes a valuable asset – you can offer replays to those who couldn't attend live and repurpose the content into blog posts, social media snippets, or even email marketing campaigns.

Finally, knowledge is power. Zoom Webinar provides robust analytics that can shed light on attendee behavior during your workshops. These insights, such as attendance rates, participation in polls and Q&A, and session completion data, offer valuable feedback on the effectiveness of your content and presentation style. By analyzing this data, you can identify areas for improvement, tailor future workshops to better address audience needs, and ultimately ensure your workshops deliver maximum value for both you and your potential clients.

If you plan on hosting webinars, choosing a platform like Zoom Webinar is an investment in the future of your estate planning practice.

Email Marketing: Don't Be Forgotten!

I can't emphasize enough how important staying top of mind is for estate planning lawyers. The simple reality is that many people are not ready to hire you right away. Someone who just got rear-ended and now has back problems is ready to hire a personal injury attorney. Someone who just got their third DUI is ready to hire a third-offense DUI attorney. Most estate planning prospects simply do not have the same sense of urgency. That's okay, but it doesn't mean you want to disappear! **With automated email drip campaigns, you can both educate and provide value in a way that keeps you front and center when they are ready to move forward.** People will opt in, and if they don't want to hear from you anymore, they'll simply unsubscribe.

There are many email marketing tools that allow you to segment your audiences using "tags" and send targeted, automated emails to each group. Some options include Mailchimp, Constant Contact, and Active Campaign. Sample tags could be "estate planning lead," "seminar attendee," "seminar no-show," or "estate planning client." Each group needs different messaging and should have a different Call To Action (CTA). Estate planning leads, for example, should be part of a New Contact Nurture Campaign, with emails designed to educate and stay top of mind. The CTA could be to register for a webinar, book a consultation, or follow your firm on Instagram. A webinar attendee should be getting emails encouraging them to book a consultation. A webinar no-show should be getting emails encouraging them to watch the limited-time replay. And an estate planning client should be getting emails related to their matter and goings-on with the firm.

Never underestimate the power of staying in touch with your leads. I've had people contact me years after attending a workshop or consultation, saying they weren't ready at the time, but now they are. It's always a pleasant surprise when you get that email: "We're ready to move forward with our estate plan! Who should we make the check out to?" It's business I might have lost if I hadn't maintained those connections.

The moral of the story? Build your email list. Every lead, business contact, and client should be added to your audience and tagged appropriately. **An audience built on Instagram or Facebook can go away overnight with a tweak of the algorithm. Your email list is YOURS. It is an asset you own and control. Build it and use it wisely.**

Skillful use of technology takes every element of the ACE model and automates it.

Again, this is a Mindset shift from a lawyer who uses software to an entrepreneur who provides legal services. Automation in all the right places frees you as the attorney up to hone your most valuable skills: building relationships and practicing law.

Isn't This a Bit Standoffish?

I hear occasionally on discovery calls that this model is too impersonal. Your market may prefer a more personal touch, but **let's take a step back from another common Mindset issue: all-or-nothing thinking**. Although some clients may lack the technological experience to complete an intake questionnaire or book online, it doesn't hurt to offer the option to those who do have it. It's simply an experiment in how you run your business. Set up the Tech Stack and see how different client demographics respond, keeping in mind that we only recommend technology we know will save you time.

When Andres implemented these and other software tools, he not only found hours each week but also increased peace of mind. He worried less about making sure clients were scheduled and felt relieved to know he only had to explain documents live to clients who weren't comfortable with watching videos online. Those found hours and the attention he reclaimed gave him more capacity to diversify his marketing efforts, enjoy time with his friends, and, best of all, recommit to his art.

You Have to Spend Money to Make Money

I've only scratched the surface of the software tools 2HLL suggests to buy back time. The key word here is "buy." As I stated at the beginning of this chapter, you have to spend money to start a business. Think of it as an investment, not an expense. **These tools are designed to free up your precious time, allowing you to focus on the high-value activities that drive growth and revenue (and get to your version of the ballet on a Tuesday afternoon).** Imagine reclaiming hours you used to spend on administrative tasks and instead dedicating that time to building client relationships, developing marketing strategies, or focusing on strategic business development. The return on investment from these tools can be significant, multiplying your productivity and ultimately contributing to your bottom line. Remember, time is your most valuable resource, and these software solutions can empower you to "buy back" time and invest it in the areas that will propel your business forward.

EXERCISE:

1. How is your current technology setup serving you? Sabotaging you? What feels like a doable experiment to run?
2. What are your practice's pain points? Is there a technology that would alleviate some of the frustration?
3. What is it worth to you to get out of a practice that's not serving you and into one that is?

The Enemy Part of Frenemy

Now that I've talked about all the ways technology can support your entrepreneurial efforts, I would be remiss if I didn't mention all the ways technology is currently sabotaging your entrepreneurial efforts, as well as the rest of your life.

The statistics regarding the number of hours spent on your phone, tablet, or laptop are demoralizing. **If you feel like you're addicted to your phone in general and the apps on that phone in particular, it's because you are.** In *Digital Minimalism*, Cal Newport explains how technology companies have engineered the phone and the apps on it in the same way that gambling organizations have engineered every single table and machine on the casino floor. The principle is simple and very well understood in the realm of human psychology: human beings engage more with actions that provide intermittent positive reinforcement. The same principle holds true for other mammals: rats are more likely to press levers to get a food pellet if a food pellet is delivered randomly. We watch sports or play games because we don't know whether or not we're going to win; when we do know what's coming, we're less likely to want to continue playing.

Intermittent positive reinforcement — the principle behind every social media app on your phone — leads to obsessive behavior.

It feels counterintuitive, but there is an evolutionary advantage to this behavior. Randomly finding berries ensured our ancestors on the savannah would continue to search for berries, an important trait when survival meant you'd get your genes into the next generation.

The problem with apps like Facebook, Instagram, and sites like Reddit is that we don't know what we're going to find when we log in and start scrolling. We do know it's likely we'll find something that will either amuse or outrage us. But whereas gambling with your dollars produces an obvious negative in the way your bank account decreases or your debt increases, gambling with your time and attention produces less obvious and measurable disadvantages, less concrete in terms of damage. Many people end up in a middle ground where their business, relationships, and free time activities aren't as meaningful as they could be, but they're also not so bad that the consequences require action because time, attention, and relationships are elastic and can absorb repeated hits.

You feel harried all the time like there isn't enough time in the day.

You're distracted, so you're impatient with the people in your life.

You work in a cycle that means things get done, but not with an attention that generates a sense of satisfaction with the result.

Remember Newport's argument that satisfaction at work depends less on your "passion" or the content of your work and more on less tangible traits like autonomy, impact, and connection? Reducing the amount of time you spend in activities that sabotage all three of these traits may go a long way toward boosting your happiness without having to leave the law.

BONUS EXERCISE:

For a minimum of one week:

1. Develop a plan to reduce the amount of time you spend on your devices. This includes social media, news websites, and digital streaming services.
2. Check your email to 2 or 3 designed times each day. Inform your staff, if you have one, of this new experiment. Set up an auto-reply on your email with links to book an appointment and information on when to expect a response.
3. Replace that activity with a walk outside, a hobby you've neglected, or a book or puzzle.
4. Note how you feel.

AI: The Elephant in the Room

But, you say, but! But what about the elephant in the room? **What about AI? AI is coming for our jobs!**

Maybe. Just as I don't have a time machine enabling us to go back and make different choices, I also don't have a crystal ball enabling us to see what the future holds. What I can state, with total confidence, is that avoiding engaging with technology leads to a sense of helplessness and frustration.

Let's start by breaking down what AI is. In simple terms, artificial intelligence involves using computers to perform tasks that usually require human intelligence. The goal is to create machines that can "think" like humans. AI enables computers to carry out tasks we would typically consider "smart," like processing vast amounts of data quickly — something humans struggle to do. It can also simulate some cognitive functions, like learning from data, problem-solving, and making decisions based on that information. A good example is ChatGPT. Although it doesn't replicate human consciousness, it uses data to learn and respond intelligently.

There's a lot of talk about how AI will take over jobs, even in the legal profession, with some predicting that in a few years, AI will replace us, and we'll all be out on the streets. **Personally, I don't believe this doomsday scenario**. This is not a new problem — it's just another iteration of a challenge attorneys have faced for years: low-cost or free alternatives that claim to offer the same outcome as a lawyer, but at a fraction of the price.

First, it was the DIY approach, with people writing their own wills. Then came will and trust templates from bookstores, where you'd "fill in the blanks" and hope for the best. Next, platforms like LegalZoom appeared, spreading the myth that complex legal matters could be handled with a few clicks. More recently, financial advisors and other non-attorneys entered the space, offering their own versions of estate planning. This feels particularly concerning when clients who said "no" to LegalZoom might say "yes" to their trusted financial advisor.

Now, AI has entered the scene. So, what's next?

As a practicing estate planning attorney, let me start by saying I completely understand these concerns. Like you, I earn a living selling estate planning services to my community. I, too, worry about what will happen if clients stop hiring lawyers and start creating their wills on ChatGPT or ditch us for the guy doing their taxes. I'm not here to downplay the issue or ignore valid concerns. Instead, I'm here to tell you there's a solution.

Before diving into the client service model we teach our members that ensures they'll never be replaced, let's establish some facts:

First, non-lawyers and tech solutions have always tried to break into our space. From DIY will kits and online software to financial advisors, there have been repeated attempts to take a share of our market. **LegalZoom has been trying to disrupt the industry for 25 years, offering low-cost wills and trusts, yet here we are, still with thriving estate planning practices**. This shows that many consumers are rejecting those alternatives, even with their lower costs.

Second, clients will always need legal expertise, not generic solutions. AI and financial advisors might be appealing for their simplicity or convenience, but estate planning isn't a "plug-and-play" process. Clients need expert legal guidance tailored to their unique situations. **Complex issues, changing laws, and intricate family dynamics all require the counsel, expertise, and care of an estate planning attorney**. No other solution can compete with that.

Lastly, clients value long-term counsel, not quick fixes. AI-generated estate plans or a brief consultation with a financial advisor might seem attractive at first, but estate planning is an ongoing relationship. Laws change, family dynamics shift, and clients need long-term support to keep their plans current. By emphasizing the value of a long-term relationship, you show clients why working with you is far better than relying on quick, impersonal solutions.

Now, you might be thinking, "I know this is true, but my clients don't!"

Tell them!

The problem hasn't changed, and neither has the solution: educating your community through seminars and webinars so they understand (1) the problems estate planning solves, and (2) why these problems are best handled by an estate planning attorney — not ChatGPT. That's why Education is a core value of 2-Hour Lifestyle Lawyer, and it will remain that way. **An attorney who prioritizes Education and Relationships in their practice will never be replaced.**

So, go ahead and use AI and other tools in your law firm, but rest assured they won't replace you. **Like Dorothy, you already have everything you need.**

In the final chapter, I'll talk about how hiring an effective team helps you both buy back time and reclaim your eyeballs from the slot machine in your pocket or purse.

Chapter Summary

- Effective use of technology is a vital, necessary part of your practice.
- 2HLL's tested and vetted technology recommendations offer a number of ways to buy back your time, take the repetition and inefficiency out of your workflows, and free you up to pursue your interests and hobbies.
- Examining and refining your relationship with non-practice-related websites and apps also frees up time and energy.
- AI is not coming for your job, but the AI-educated attorney who engages with and masters this technology is. Be that attorney.

Seven
Even Solos Need a Team

Our 2HLLs had lots to say about the struggles business owners face when hiring, training, and utilizing their staff:

- "I have a team. **None of them are working in the way I need them to work** but I can't seem to let them go, or get them doing what I actually need done. I'm sure that's partly my fault."
- "I'm not sure how to go about hiring an assistant. An in-person assistant is too expensive for me, but how can I trust that a virtual assistant is actually doing what I need done?"
- "I can't manage myself and my own work. **How am I going to manage someone else?"**

People. People, people, people. The good fits fill our lives with efficiency, confidence, connection, and value. Bad fits are a drain on your time, your energy, and your bottom line.

In the previous chapter on technology, I talked about how technology can serve you as a lawyer-entrepreneur. But many solo lawyers, tech-savvy or not, when faced with the complexity of online marketing efforts, scheduling software, and webinar technologies, just to name a few, mentally shut down and implement none of them.

The Solution? Hire Someone Else to Do It

Let me share a little secret with you: as an attorney, you shouldn't be doing everything in your law firm, even if you're just starting out. Sure, you might be able to answer the phone, create marketing materials, or manage the books, but that's not why you went to law school. **Your focus should be on practicing law, not perfecting your Canva skills.** If you want to thrive in both your career and personal life, it's crucial to start delegating tasks that don't require your expertise.

Consider your experience at a doctor's office. Does your doctor personally answer the phone to schedule your appointment? Do they hand you the forms when you arrive, take your weight and blood pressure, or follow up on overdue bills? Of course not. Your doctor delegates these tasks to others so they can focus on what truly matters: practicing medicine.

It's the same in the legal profession. Somewhere along the line, the idea took hold that being a good attorney means doing everything yourself. I often hear things like, "I thought being there for my clients was a good thing" or "My clients don't want an answering service; they want me!" as reasons for sticking to this outdated mindset. Now, we have a generation of attorneys who feel stuck, taking on not only their legal duties but everyone else's tasks, too. **The truth is, by trying to do it all, you're not helping your clients — you're actually doing them a disservice by spending time on administrative tasks instead of practicing law.**

The good news is that the 2HLL model doesn't require a huge staff, an expensive staff, or a staff that requires a big office downtown. One well-trained virtual assistant or paralegal is all you need to reclaim your time and your sanity.

This is a common model in the business world. Russell Brunson,[6] a thought leader in the business and personal development spaces, developed a philosophy for entrepreneurs that centers around two roles: the **Attractive Character** and the **Implementor**. In the context of estate planning, the attorney is the Attractive Character. As the Attractive Character, you present legal concepts in a clear, concise, and jargon-free manner. You can showcase your expertise and experience in crafting personalized estate plans and position yourself as a trusted guide.

The Attractive Character isn't about creating a fake persona. Far from it! Most people can smell a salesperson intent on relieving them from their credit card a mile away and will consciously avoid that person. Instead, seeing yourself as the Attractive Character provides the framework to strategically use storytelling and relatable communication to connect with your target audience and build trust. **For an estate planning attorney, the Attractive Character leverages empathy, clear communication, and a genuine desire to help families navigate the complexities of estate planning.**

The Implementor role complements this by focusing on action. Your virtual assistant's job is to help you implement it so you can get back to your job as the Attractive Character. They will take your knowledge and strategies and put them into practice. Simply providing information as the Attractive Character isn't enough; effective implementation by the Implementor is crucial for achieving your vision of success.

The ACE Framework also supports having an assistant. Per ACE, the attorney is the Attractive Character and should be focusing on networking, educating your community, and hosting client consultations. Why? Because those are the revenue-generating activities! Much of the execution can and should be done with systems, automation, and a virtual assistant Implementor. **If you want the secret to making more while working less, this is it. Hire a VA.**

6 Blankenship. Mike. "The Attractive Character: How to Build Your Own From Scratch." Click Funnels. July 14, 2022. https://www.clickfunnels.com/blog/attractive-character/

But I Can't Afford an Assistant!

Let's turn that around and ask it differently: **Can you afford NOT to get a social media presence going? Can you afford NOT to have automated email drip campaigns? Can you afford NOT to be fully utilizing technology?**

Think of it this way: You've spent years of your life and tens, if not hundreds, of thousands of dollars training and developing your skill set as a lawyer. Unless you are a person who either finds technology easy to implement or someone who genuinely enjoys the rabbit holes of efficiency and optimization, **the most effective way you can get your time back is by hiring people to do the things that don't require a law degree**. This frees up your time — whether you're charging by the billable hour or by the flat-fee model — to spend it either on things that do require a law degree, or on the Attracting and Closing portions of the 2HLL model, or with your children and partner, or your golden retriever.

Why does this matter?

For Sarah, our 2HLL who left litigation at a Big Law firm and lived in a high-cost-of-living region, tech and a part-time virtual assistant meant she could focus on the A and the C and thus close more clients each month. More clients closed consistently meant she didn't have to live with roommates. The first night she went to bed in her own apartment to silence rather than the background noise of her roommate's favorite reality TV show was one of the best nights of her life.

For Andres, implementing technology and hiring a part-time virtual assistant radically increased his life satisfaction. Yes, his paycheck from his firm took a small hit, but every time he walked into his studio space at four in the afternoon, he knew the small financial hit brought big meaning for him.

For Adam, effective support from paralegals and assistants meant more time with his rapidly growing kids. When he handed off a task and left on time, he knew he was living his values.

Take the First Step

Ask around in your network to find recommendations, or use a website like Fiverr or Upwork to widen your potential pool of candidates. Sites like these connect you with people around the world who can manage your calendar software, post to your social media accounts, and book speaking engagements, just to name a few things you can offload from your mental plate. Imagine getting an email listing all of the groups in your area who fit your target market, complete with membership numbers and contact information. How much easier would it feel to reach out to a couple each month and work on relationships, not research?

Another advantage to hiring a VA through Fiverr or Upwork is that you are not hiring a full-time employee. Offer one assignment and see how the person does. If things aren't working out in a way that supports your business, try someone else. Businesses and needs change. As I've grown 2HLL, my needs have shifted from one VA to a team of almost ten, each one easing my own burden and helping grow the business. **Acknowledging that business needs change allowed me and will allow you to iterate in the team component of your practice.**

Startup Costs

In both of these situations, there is an initial outlay of time and energy to interview, hire, and train a team member. Also, consider the effort you'll put into figuring out what you want to offload and how that integrates with your practice workflow. **Although these tasks can seem overwhelming, I have found that, when considered from a Mindset perspective, members who engage with these questions find unparalleled insights into how their practices' workflows are supporting or hindering their efforts to live the life they want to live.** You'll learn something about your practice you didn't know beforehand, which will enable you to refine your processes and find other ways to increase revenue ... or get out the door on the way home earlier.

EXERCISE:

Sometimes, feeling like you're adding yet another task to your already crammed to-do list and calendar makes it difficult to move forward. Let's reframe this: think of building your team via the power of subtracting by considering these questions:

1. What would give you the most satisfaction to subtract from your current workload?
2. What are you doing at the moment that does not require a lawyer to do? Do you know what it would cost to outsource those tasks? If not, can you block an hour or two to do some research?
3. What tasks will take Execute tasks off your plate and increase your Attract and Closing efforts to grow your bottom line? Which ones are crucial for you to do, and which ones can you outsource?
4. What do you most dread? How can you shift that to a team member who loves it?

We often think that because we don't want to do a certain task, other people don't want to do it either. We don't want to be "that person" who offloads the "crap" onto someone else. **It's helpful to remember that one person's "crap" is another person's sweet spot.** Several 2HLLs who thoroughly enjoy drafting estate plans now provide their drafting services to other 2HLLs who want to know the work is done right and are not in a place at the moment to hire a paralegal. Some 2HLLs absolutely love social media — they want to figure out the best ads for the current algorithms, do the design work, schedule the posts, and track the responses. Many others find social media overwhelming and exhausting; the good news is there are entire marketing businesses designed around the kind of social media engagement that many people dread. Hire one of those individuals and create a win-win situation for both of you.

Have a Social Media Presence ... But Don't Manage It Yourself

One additional advantage to outsourcing your social media is that it helps reduce the barrier we often feel when we think about "putting myself out there." **Members of our Lifestyle Lawyer Collective get a marketing bundle delivered straight to their inbox every month**, designed to be easy for a VA to customize and post. Members who haven't yet joined the Collective can hire someone versed in estate planning to create graphics and captions for them. In either case, all the lawyer has to do is approve the post. Ask your VA to track likes, click-throughs, and other responses and provide you with a summary. This makes the seemingly uphill battle around marketing feel more like an experiment than the intensely personal effort around "putting myself out there."

Also, in the same vein as "You are not your hourly rate," you are not putting your "self" out there. You're marketing the very necessary services you provide to your community. Your "self" is, we know, comprised of far more than your ability to create estate plans.

You Could Do It All, but Why Would You?

When people brag that they can do it all, I ask, "Sure, but why would you?" Being an entrepreneur-lawyer means that you are the absolute authority on what work you do and don't do. Outsourcing isn't a sign of weakness or ineptitude. It's a sign that you understand your business well enough to know what requires your attention and effort — and what doesn't.

Here's what 2HLLs, many of whom are solos, say about the process and benefits of refining their team:

- "I share the responsibilities of running my ... business with a co-founder, and **I have experience working with freelancers. Working with them brought flexibility and allowed me to tap into specialized skills when needed. However, it also underscored the importance of clear communication and effective project management to ensure everyone is aligned with the business's vision and objectives**. For my legal practice, I believe hiring the right help and bringing on partners could indeed make a significant difference to both my peace of mind and the success of the business." (This 2HLL already had experience as an entrepreneur.)
- "I am a solo attorney. I do have a full-time paralegal — which I had prior to 2HLL — and a part time VA, which I found because of 2HLL. **Hiring the right people for my team [has] made a huge difference in my practice.**"
- "I started the firm with my law school classmate, and he has entrusted me to make all business decisions. I still include him in my decision-making, but ultimately I make all the decisions. **I've also hired a business development person as my business manager to implement strategies to grow our firm. We got**

extremely lucky hiring our first employee. He helped us 3–5× our monthly revenue since we brought him onboard."

- "... **I know for a fact that hiring support staff lightens the load.** I already have a legal assistant I found on Upwork, and she helps me with the personal injury side of my practice."
- "I am right now a true solo but really look forward to bringing people on. **I have managed teams in my previous career and know the importance of delegating and building teams.** After I get a few clients under my belt, I would like to hire a personal assistant."
- "... I have worked in a law firm of ten lawyers or so, and also started a law firm with another lawyer, where we initially had an associate and other support staff. **I think hiring paralegals and other support staff is far more useful for a solo attorney than hiring or partnering with another attorney.**"
- "... I have learned (especially this time around having worked with assistants in the past) that **it is impossible to thrive without an assistant. The amount of time I spend doing tasks that do not utilize the benefits of my degree and institutional knowledge is vast, and that time could instead be used to both generate more business and draft more documents that bring revenue into the firm. I have both a virtual assistant and a full-time legal assistant who will likely become a paralegal starting with me this January — just shy of my one year mark in business.**"
- "... This year I hired two paralegals, an executive assistant and part-time lawyer. **Hiring the right people (meaning experienced people) is the best thing you can do.** It may seem scary but they can jump right in and take on cases without much instruction. **This allows you to make more cases and grow the firm (while also giving you time back to work ON the firm).**"

The last quote is spot on — **you hire the best, most experienced person you can find for what you need done so you can focus "on the firm."** As tired as the analogy is, it's very hard to move a business forward if you are constantly rooting around in the weeds of the tasks for which you are not trained and are yet vital to your business's growth.

Hiring and Firing

Finding the right people and learning how to delegate and manage your team isn't a skill that's taught in law school. Getting comfortable with the management role — to say nothing of gaining experience interviewing and hiring — takes time, and it comes with hiccups that offer opportunities to experiment with your staffing needs. Maybe you hired an office assistant and weren't seeing the benefits you hoped for, and what you learned was that you need a paralegal instead. After joining the Lifestyle Lawyer Collective, one member wrestled with her staffing issues and decided to consciously reduce her staff. She then hired strategically to replace them and experienced a significant shift in her mental well-being and in her practice's workflow.

It's not easy to let someone go. **What may be helpful is to compare keeping someone you know isn't the right fit for the job with what you give up by keeping that individual. If an unsuitable fit means you're staying late, checking work, or experiencing anxiety around the whole situation, that is a real cost to yourself that you can't measure in a salary.**

Again, this is an advantage to the gig economy world we live in. Offering assignments on a trial basis, explaining your expectations, discussing the results, reflecting on how it went, and practicing saying, "I appreciate you and your work, but this isn't working out for me," provides so many developmental opportunities for you as a lawyer, an entrepreneur, and a human being. Each assignment offers the opportunity to get clear on what you want and ask for it. This may feel hard, but as with most difficult things, the results are transformative for you and your practice.

Chapter Summary

Going "solo" doesn't mean you have to do everything yourself. In fact, the opposite! Delegating appropriately is essential to preserving your work-life balance and the lifestyle you want. Consider these tips:

- Outsource what doesn't require a law degree to free up time and energy for attracting and closing business.
- A virtual assistant can take on many of the daily repetitive tasks, freeing up valuable time for you.
- Social media outreach is another area that can be handled more easily by a marketing professional — freeing up not just time but also removing stress about putting your "self" out there.
- The gig economy and sites like Fiverr and Upwork take the hassle out of finding and hiring people.

Visit lifestylelawyerrevolution.com for free resources!

Part Two Capstone Exercise:

Return to your original Why. Again, let's remember what Cal Newport's research told him about satisfaction at work. **The content of your work and whether or not you were "passionate" about it did not correlate or cause satisfaction to go up. Autonomy, impact, and connection all made notable differences in work satisfaction, not passion.**

1. How well is your work supporting your Why?
2. What have you realized or understood while working through the book's exercises?
3. Are you and your values being served in your current work?
4. Look through the exercises in Part Two. What feels like a step you can take to move forward?
5. How can you make your practice fit you and your needs rather than your practice and your career running you?
6. Where are you working from anxiety rather than confidence?
7. What anxiety-inducing tasks could you take off your plate?
8. What could you add (or subtract!) that would boost your confidence?
9. What would increase your sense of autonomy, of contribution, of connection?

Are you ready to start creating that vision today?!

Visit lifestylelawyerrevolution.com for free resources!

Take Big Steps

Let others lead small lives, but not you. Let others argue over small things, but not you. Let others cry over small hurts, but not you. Let others leave their future in someone else's hands, but not you. And remember, the four things that never return: the spoken word, the speeding arrow, the wasted life, and the neglected opportunity.
— Jim Rohn

The reason most people fail instead of succeed is they trade what they want most for what they want at the moment.
— Napoleon Bonaparte

I've mentioned elements of my story throughout this book. There's one more story I'd like to share that's the foundation of my success — and can be yours, too. It's about my very first memory and how it changed the way I think forever.

My older sisters and I were all born at the same hospital in Halifax, Nova Scotia, in the 1970s. We lived with my parents, Ann and Jim, on a beautiful sloping tree-lined street. One end led down to Halifax Harbor, and the other end led up to a big hill. One winter day when I was about four years old, my father took us all sledding. I was the youngest, smallest child hiking back up a very steep, snowy hill, and I kept falling behind.

"Wait for me!" I called.

Without pausing, my father turned back to me and said, "Take big steps, Laura."

Take big steps.

Big steps when you're four years old are actually small steps, proving the old adage that size, indeed, does not matter. What mattered was that, small step by small step, I got the big win of getting up the hill in deep Canadian winter snow, under my own power, so I could slide back down again.

That moment in my life planted the seed of Grit that I could deliver newspapers in scorching Iowa summers and freezing winters to fund my ballet lessons. That I could study accounting and become a CPA. That I could move to New York City with no family or friends, trying out different jobs with different companies. That I could pivot to becoming an executive assistant for high-net-worth individuals, pivot again to go to law school, recover from being fired, and pivot yet again to open my own law firm. And in 2022, I pivoted yet again when the constellations of stars comprising my work experience, my education, and my business experience coalesced into the 2-Hour Lifestyle Lawyer.

Remember the zeroes. Metaphorically speaking, those zeroes are the Canadian winter snow of life.

What Are Your Small Steps and Your Big Wins?

My final exercise is to ask you to think about your own "big" steps. Then pull out a brand new legal pad – because this list is going to get long – and write "My Never-Ending List of Wins" at the top. **Where have you persevered to succeed (or simply not fail — that's a win) in your life?**

- Graduating from law school and passing the bar automatically goes on the list, but dig deeper into your past and your heart than that.
- Do you remember the sense of pride you felt when you first traversed the entire section of monkey bars on the playground? Turned a cartwheel? Dug a deep hole in the sandbox? Add that to the list.
- Didn't make a team, practiced, and made it the next year? Goes on the list. (Think Michael Jordan not making varsity his sophomore year).
- Didn't make the team, tried a different sport or extracurricular, and found something you actually enjoy? Goes on the list.
- Did you ask for something you needed (doesn't matter if you got it)? Speak up for yourself.
- Did you take time for yourself when it felt like insubordination or even rebellion? Put it on the list.
- Studied your way into a decent grade in a subject that didn't come naturally to you? Learn a hobby you thought you couldn't? Slap that on the list.
- Learned a new practice area? Survived your first court appearance? Got better as a trial attorney? Wrote a stellar brief? Fought a good fight for someone and won?
- What thanks, compliments, and expressions of gratitude have you received from clients? Put them on the list.
- Faced a fear again and again until you overcame it? Top of the list.

Once you have a solid list — at least a page — take some time and reflect back on these experiences. What motivated you? How did determination or Grit feel in your heart and body? How can that felt sense translate into the confidence to make the law work for you rather than the other way around?

If you found even the tiniest bit of Grit inside you and wrote down even one win, you're ready to join almost 500 and counting determined, energized, and supportive lawyers on the 2HLL journey because there's one more benefit to joining 2HLL: our community.

When you join 2HLL as a lawyer-entrepreneur, you get a built-in network of connections to other lawyer-entrepreneurs you can support and feel supported by in turn. This goes a long way towards making the journey feel like a fun road trip — with snacks! — rather than a grueling endurance race through the mud and over obstacles. I'm very proud of the supportive and engaged 2HLL community, built and nurtured by my values of Community and Positivity, and supported by coaches who guide estate planning novices through learning a new practice area and who offer diverse programs and courses to support Mindset and business development, from one-to-one sessions through courses targeting specific speed bumps like boundaries, the inner critic, and imposter syndrome. Joining the Lifestyle Lawyer Collective membership provides accountability, a place to brainstorm about roadblocks and next steps, a way to share experiences and lessons learned, and tons of additional support as you build a life you love without leaving the law.

JOIN US!!!

Visit www.2HourLifestyleLawyer.com

Author Bio

Laura E. Cowan, Esq., is the Founder of the Law Office of Laura Cowan, a boutique estate planning firm located in the heart of New York City. She graduated from Iowa State University with a degree in Accounting and subsequently passed the CPA Exam. After working for companies such as Ernst + Young and Goldman Sachs, Laura attended the University of Minnesota Law School, graduating in 2013. She launched her firm in 2016, building it to seven figures in less than three years. In March of 2020, Laura turned her award-winning practice entirely virtual. Laura created 2-Hour Lifestyle Lawyer™ in 2022 to teach other lawyers how to build a five-star estate planning practice they can run from anywhere. In 2023, Laura launched the Lifestyle Lawyer Collective™, an ongoing membership that supports graduates of our course with marketing, coaching, and implementation. Still a practicing attorney, Laura lives in New York City and enjoys running in Central Park and going to the New York City Ballet.

Laura can be reached at Laura@2HourLifestyleLawyer.com.

Are you ready to join the Lifestyle Lawyer Revolution? Book a Discovery Call today!

www.2HourLifestyleLawyer.com

Made in the USA
Monee, IL
13 September 2026

62981868R00089